THE ANCIEN REGIME

Charles Kingsley

1st WORLD
LIBRARY
Literary Society

The Ancien Regime

Charles Kingsley

© 1st World Library – Literary Society, 2004
PO Box 2211
Fairfield, IA 52556
www.1stworldlibrary.org
First Edition

LCCN: 2004091168

Softcover ISBN: 1-59540-614-X
eBook ISBN: 1-59540-714-6

The Ancien Regime
contributed by the Charles Family
in support of
1st World Library Literary Society

PREFACE

The rules of the Royal Institution forbid (and wisely) religious or political controversy. It was therefore impossible for me in these Lectures, to say much which had to be said, in drawing a just and complete picture of the Ancien Regime in France. The passages inserted between brackets, which bear on religious matters, were accordingly not spoken at the Royal Institution.

But more. It was impossible for me in these Lectures, to bring forward as fully as I could have wished, the contrast between the continental nations and England, whether now, or during the eighteenth century. But that contrast cannot be too carefully studied at the present moment. In proportion as it is seen and understood, will the fear of revolution (if such exists) die out among the wealthier classes; and the wish for it (if such exists) among the poorer; and a large extension of the suffrage will be looked on as - what it actually is - a safe and harmless concession to the wishes - and, as I hold, to the just rights - of large portion of the British nation.

There exists in Britain now, as far as I can see, no one of those evils which brought about the French Revolution. There is no widespread misery, and therefore no widespread discontent, among the classes who live by hand-labour. The legislation of the last generation has been steadily in favour of the poor, as against the rich; and it is even more true now than it was in 1789, that - as Arthur Young told the French mob which stopped his carriage - the rich pay many taxes (over and above the poor-rates, a direct tax on the capitalist in favour of the labourer) more than are paid by the poor. "In England" (says M. de Tocqueville of even the eighteenth century) "the poor man enjoyed the privilege of exemption from taxation; in France, the rich." Equality before the law is as well-nigh complete as it can be, where some are rich and others poor; and the only privileged class, it sometimes seems to me, is the pauper, who has neither the responsibility of self-government, nor the toil of self-support.

A minority of malcontents, some justly, some unjustly, angry with the present state of things, will always exist in this world. But a majority of malcontents we shall never have, as long as the workmen are allowed to keep untouched and unthreatened their rights of free speech, free public meeting, free combination for all purposes which do not provoke a breach of the peace. There may be (and probably are) to be found in London and the large towns, some of those revolutionary propagandists who have terrified and tormented continental statesmen since the year 1815. But they are far fewer in number than in 1848; far fewer still (I believe) than in 1831; and their habits, notions, temper, whole mental organisation, is so utterly alien to that of the average Englishman, that it is only the sense of wrong which can make him take counsel with them, or make common cause with them. Meanwhile, every man who is admitted to a vote, is one more person withdrawn from the temptation to disloyalty, and enlisted in maintaining the powers that be - when they are in the wrong, as well as when they are in the right. For every Englishman is by his nature conservative; slow to form an opinion; cautious in putting it into effect; patient under evils which seem irremediable; persevering in abolishing such as seem remediable; and then only too ready to acquiesce in the earliest practical result; to "rest and be thankful." His faults, as well as his virtues, make him anti-revolutionary. He is generally too dull to take in a great idea; and if he does take it in, often too selfish to apply it to any interest save his own. But now and then, when the sense of actual injury forces upon him a great idea, like that of Free-trade or of Parliamentary Reform, he is indomitable, however slow and patient, in translating his thought into fact: and they will not be wise statesmen who resist his dogged determination. If at this moment he demands an extension of the suffrage eagerly and even violently, the wise statesman will give at once, gracefully and generously, what the Englishman will certainly obtain one day, if he has set his mind upon it. If, on the other hand, he asks for it calmly, then the wise statesman (instead of mistaking English reticence for apathy) will listen to his wishes all the more readily; seeing in the moderation of the demand, the best possible guarantee for moderation in the use of the thing demanded.

And, be it always remembered, that in introducing these men into the "balance of the Constitution," we introduce no unknown quantity. Statesmen ought to know them, if they know themselves; to judge what the working man would do by what they do themselves. He who imputes virtues to his own class imputes them also to the labouring class. He who imputes vices to the labouring class, imputes them to his own class. For both are not only of the same flesh and blood, but, what is infinitely more important, of the same spirit; of the same race; in innumerable cases, of the same ancestors. For centuries past the most able of these men have been working upwards into the middle class, and through it, often, to the highest dignities, and the highest family connections; and the whole nation knows how they have comported themselves therein. And, by a reverse process (of which the physiognomist and genealogist can give abundant proof), the weaker members of that class which was dominant during the Middle Age have been sinking downward, often to the rank of mere day-labourers, and carrying downward with them - sometimes in a very tragical and pathetic fashion - somewhat of the dignity and the refinement which they had learnt from their ancestors.

Thus has the English nation (and as far as I can see, the Scotch likewise) become more homogeneous than any nation of the Continent, if we except France since the extermination of the Frankish nobility. And for that very reason, as it seems to me, it is more fitted than any other European nation for the exercise of equal political rights; and not to be debarred of them by arguments drawn from countries which have been governed - as England has not been - by a caste.

The civilisation, not of mere book-learning, but of the heart; all that was once meant by "manners" - good breeding, high feeling, respect for self and respect for others - are just as common (as far as I have seen) among the hand-workers of England and Scotland, as among any other class; the only difference is, that these qualities develop more early in the richer classes, owing to that severe discipline of our public schools, which makes mere lads often fit to govern, because they have learnt to obey: while they develop later -

generally not till middle age - in the classes who have not gone through in their youth that Spartan training, and who indeed (from a mistaken conception of liberty) would not endure it for a day. This and other social drawbacks which are but too patent, retard the manhood of the working classes. That it should be so, is a wrong. For if a citizen have one right above all others to demand anything of his country, it is that he should be educated; that whatever capabilities he may have in him, however small, should have their fair and full chance of development. But the cause of the wrong is not the existence of a caste, or a privileged class, or of anything save the plain fact, that some men will be always able to pay more for their children's education than others; and that those children will, inevitably, win in the struggle of life.

Meanwhile, in this fact is to be found the most weighty, if not the only argument against manhood suffrage, which would admit many - but too many, alas! - who are still mere boys in mind. To a reasonable household suffrage it cannot apply. The man who (being almost certainly married, and having children) can afford to rent a 5 pound tenement in a town, or in the country either, has seen quite enough of life, and learnt quite enough of it, to form a very fair judgment of the man who offers to represent him in Parliament; because he has learnt, not merely something of his own interest, or that of his class, but - what is infinitely more important - the difference between the pretender and the honest man.

The causes of this state of society, which is peculiar to Britain, must be sought far back in the ages. It would seem that the distinction between "earl and churl" (the noble and the non-noble freeman) was crushed out in this island by the two Norman conquests - that of the Anglo-Saxon nobility by Sweyn and Canute; and that of the Anglo-Danish nobility by William and his Frenchmen. Those two terrible calamities, following each other in the short space of fifty years, seem to have welded together, by a community of suffering, all ranks and races, at least south of the Tweed; and when the English rose after the storm, they rose as one homogeneous people, never to be governed again by an originally alien race. The English nobility were, from the time of Magna Charta, rather an official nobility, than, as in most continental countries, a separate caste; and whatever caste tendencies had developed themselves before the Wars of the Roses (as such are certain to do during centuries of continued wealth and power), were crushed out by the great revolutionary events of the next hundred years. Especially did the discovery of the New World, the maritime struggle with Spain, the outburst of commerce and colonisation during the reigns of Elizabeth and James, help toward this good result. It was in vain for the Lord Oxford of the day, sneering at Raleigh's sudden elevation, to complain that as on the virginals, so in the State, "Jacks went up, and heads went down." The proudest noblemen were not ashamed to have their ventures on the high seas, and to send their younger sons trading, or buccaneering, under the conduct of low-born men like Drake, who "would like to see the gentleman that would not set his hand to a rope, and hale and draw with the mariners." Thus sprang up that respect for, even fondness for, severe bodily labour, which the educated class of no nation save our own has ever felt; and which has stood them in such good stead, whether at home or abroad. Thus, too, sprang up the system of society by which (as the ballad sets forth) the squire's son might be a "'prentice good," and marry

"The bailiff's daughter dear
That dwelt at Islington,"

without tarnishing, as he would have done on the Continent, the scutcheon of his ancestors. That which has saved England from a central despotism, such as crushed, during the eighteenth century, every nation on the Continent, is the very same peculiarity which makes the advent of the masses to a share in political power safe and harmless; namely, the absence of caste, or rather (for there is sure to be a moral fact underlying and causing every political fact) the absence of that wicked pride which perpetuates caste; forbidding those to intermarry whom nature and fact pronounce to be fit mates before God and man.

These views are not mine only. They have been already set forth so much more forcibly by M. de Tocqueville, that I should have thought it unnecessary to talk about them, were not the rhetorical phrases, "Caste," "Privileged Classes," "Aristocratic Exclusive-ness," and such-like, bandied about again just now, as if they represented facts. If there remain in this kingdom any facts which correspond to those words, let them be abolished as speedily as possible: but that such do remain was not the opinion of the master of modern political philosophy, M. de Tocqueville.

He expresses his surprise "that the fact which distinguishes England from all other modern nations, and which alone can throw light on her peculiarities, . . has not attracted more attention, . . . and that habit has rendered it, as it were, imperceptible to the English themselves - that England was the only country in which the system of caste had been not only modified, but effectually destroyed. The nobility and the middle classes followed the same business, embraced the same professions, and, what is far more significant, inter-married with each other. The daughter of the greatest nobleman" (and this, if true of the eighteenth century, has become far more true of the nineteenth) "could already, without disgrace, marry a man of yesterday." .

"It has often been remarked that the English nobility has been more prudent, more able, and less exclusive than any other. It would have been much nearer the truth to say, that in England, for a very long time past, no nobility, properly so called, have existed, if we take the word in the ancient and limited sense it has everywhere else retained." . . .

"For several centuries the word 'gentleman'" (he might have added, "burgess") "has altogether changed its meaning in England; and the word 'roturier' has ceased to exist. In each succeeding century it is applied to persons placed somewhat lower in the social scale" (as the "bagman" of Pickwick has become, and has deserved to become, the "commercial gentleman" of our day). "At length it travelled with the English to America, where it is used to designate every citizen indiscriminately. Its history is that of democracy itself." . . .

"If the middle classes of England, instead of making war upon the aristocracy, have remained so intimately connected with it, it is not especially because the aristocracy is open to all, but rather, because its outline was indistinct, and its limit unknown: not so much because any man might be admitted into it, as because it was impossible to say with certainty when he took rank there: so that all who approached it might look on themselves as belonging to it; might take part in its rule, and derive either lustre or profit from its influence."

Just so; and therefore the middle classes of Britain, of whatever their special political party, are conservative in the best sense of that word.

For there are not three, but only two, classes in England; namely, rich and poor: those who live by capital (from the wealthiest landlord to the smallest village shopkeeper); and those who live by hand-labour. Whether the division between those two classes is increasing or not, is a very serious question. Continued legislation in favour of the hand-labourer, and a beneficence towards him, when in need, such as no other nation on earth has ever shown, have done much to abolish the moral division. But the social division has surely been increased during the last half century, by the inevitable tendency, both in commerce and agriculture, to employ one large capital, where several small ones would have been employed a century ago. The large manufactory, the large shop, the large estate, the large farm, swallows up the small ones. The yeoman, the thrifty squatter who could work at two or three trades as well as till his patch of moor, the hand-loom weaver, the skilled village craftsman, have all but disappeared. The handworker, finding it more and more difficult to invest his savings, has been more and more tempted to squander them. To rise to the dignity of a capitalist, however small, was growing impossible to him, till the rise of that co-operative movement, which will do more than any social or political impulse in our day for the safety of English society, and the loyalty of the English working classes.

And meanwhile - ere that movement shall have spread throughout the length and breadth of the land, and have been applied, as it surely will be some day, not only to distribution, not only to manufacture, but to agriculture likewise - till then, the best judges of the working men's worth must be their employers; and especially the employers of the northern manufacturing population. What their judgment is, is sufficiently notorious. Those who depend most on the working men, who have the best opportunities of knowing them, trust them most thoroughly. As long as great manufacturers stand forward as the political sponsors of their own workmen, it behoves those who cannot have had their experience, to consider their opinion as conclusive. As for that "influence of the higher classes" which is said to be endangered just now; it will exist, just as much as it deserves to exist. Any man who is superior to the many, whether in talents, education, refinement, wealth, or anything else, will always be able to influence a number of men - and if he thinks it worth his while, of votes - by just and lawful means. And as for unjust and unlawful means, let those who prefer them keep up heart. The world will go on much as it did before; and be always quite bad enough to allow bribery and corruption, jobbery and nepotism, quackery and arrogance, their full influence over our home and foreign policy. An extension of the suffrage, however wide, will not bring about the millennium. It will merely make a large number of Englishmen contented and loyal, instead of discontented and disloyal. It may make, too, the educated and wealthy classes wiser by awakening a wholesome fear - perhaps, it may be, by awakening a chivalrous emulation. It may put the younger men of the present aristocracy upon their mettle, and stir them up to prove that they are not in the same effete condition as was the French noblesse in 1789. It may lead them to take the warnings which have been addressed to them, for the last thirty years, by their truest friends - often by kinsmen of their own. It may lead them to ask themselves why, in a world which is governed by a just God, such great power as is palpably theirs at present is entrusted to them, save that they may do more work, and not less, than other men, under the penalties pronounced against those to whom much is given, and of whom much is required. It may lead them to discover that they are in a world where it is not safe to sit under the tree, and let the ripe fruit drop into your mouth; where the "competition of species" works with ruthless energy among all ranks of being, from kings upon their thrones to the weeds upon the waste; where "he that is not hammer, is sure to be anvil;" and he who will not work, neither shall he eat. It may lead them to devote that energy (in which they surpass so far the continental aristocracies) to something better than outdoor amusements or indoor dilettantisms. There are those among them who, like one section of the old French noblesse, content themselves with mere complaints of "the revolutionary tendencies of the age." Let them beware in time; for when the many are on the march, the few who stand still are certain to be walked over. There are those among them who, like another section of the French noblesse, are ready, more generously than wisely, to throw away their own social and political advantages, and play (for it will never be really more than playing) at democracy. Let them, too, beware. The penknife and the axe should respect each other; for they were wrought from the same steel: but the penknife will not be wise in trying to fell trees. Let them accept their own position, not in conceit and arrogance, but in fear and trembling; and see if they cannot play the man therein, and save their own class; and with it, much which it has needed many centuries to accumulate and to organise, and without which no nation has yet existed for a single century. They are no more like the old French noblesse, than are the commercial class like the old French bourgeoisie, or the labouring like the old French peasantry. Let them prove that fact by their deeds during the next generation; or sink into the condition of mere rich men, exciting, by their luxury and laziness, nothing but envy and contempt.

Meanwhile, behind all classes and social forces - I had almost said, above them all - stands a fourth estate, which will, ultimately, decide the form which English society is to take: a Press as different from the literary class of the Ancien Regime as is everything else English; and different in this - that it is free.

The French Revolution, like every revolution (it seems to me) which has convulsed the nations of Europe for the last eighty years, was caused immediately - whatever may have been its more remote causes - by the suppression of thought; or, at least, by a sense of wrong among those who thought. A country where every man, be he fool or wise, is free to speak that which is in him, can never suffer a revolution. The folly blows itself off like steam, in harmless noise; the wisdom becomes part of the general intellectual stock of the nation, and prepares men for gradual, and therefore for harmless, change.

As long as the press is free, a nation is guaranteed against sudden and capricious folly, either from above or from below. As long as the press is free, a nation is guaranteed against the worse evil of persistent and obstinate folly, cloaking itself under the venerable shapes of tradition and authority. For under a free press, a nation must ultimately be guided not by a caste, not by a class, not by mere wealth, not by the passions of a mob: but by mind; by the net result of all the common-sense of its members; and in the present default of genius, which is un-common sense, common-sense seems to be the only, if not the best, safeguard for poor humanity.

1867

LECTURE I - CASTE

[Delivered at the Royal Institution, London, 1867.]

These Lectures are meant to be comments on the state of France before the French Revolution. To English society, past or present, I do not refer. For reasons which I have set forth at length in an introductory discourse, there never was any Ancien Regime in England.

Therefore, when the Stuarts tried to establish in England a system which might have led to a political condition like that of the Continent, all classes combined and exterminated them; while the course of English society went on as before.

On the contrary, England was the mother of every movement which undermined, and at last destroyed, the Ancien Regime.

From England went forth those political theories which, transmitted from America to France, became the principles of the French Revolution. From England went forth the philosophy of Locke, with all its immense results. It is noteworthy, that when Voltaire tries to persuade people, in a certain famous passage, that philosophers do not care to trouble the world - of the ten names to whom he does honour, seven names

Charles Kingsley

are English. "It is," he says, "neither Montaigne, nor Locke, nor Boyle, nor Spinoza, nor Hobbes, nor Lord Shaftesbury, nor Mr. Collins, nor Mr. Toland, nor Fludd, nor Baker, who have carried the torch of discord into their countries." It is worth notice, that not only are the majority of these names English, but that they belong not to the latter but to the former half of the eighteenth century; and indeed, to the latter half of the seventeenth.

So it was with that Inductive Physical Science, which helped more than all to break up the superstitions of the Ancien Regime, and to set man face to face with the facts of the universe. From England, towards the end of the seventeenth century, it was promulgated by such men as Newton, Boyle, Sydenham, Ray, and the first founders of our Royal Society.

In England, too, arose the great religious movements of the seventeenth and eighteenth centuries - and especially that of a body which I can never mention without most deep respect - the Society of Friends. At a time when the greater part of the Continent was sunk in spiritual sleep, these men were reasserting doctrines concerning man, and his relation to his Creator, which, whether or not all believe them (as I believe them) to be founded on eternal fact, all must confess to have been of incalculable benefit to the cause of humanity and civilisation.

From England, finally, about the middle of the eighteenth century, went forth - promulgated by English noblemen - that freemasonry which seems to have been the true parent of all the secret societies of Europe. Of this curious question, more hereafter. But enough has been said to show that England, instead of falling, at any period, into the stagnation of the Ancien Regime, was, from the middle of the seventeenth century, in a state of intellectual growth and ferment which communicated itself finally to the continental nations. This is the special honour of England; universally confessed at the time. It was to England that the slowly-awakening nations looked, as the source of all which was noble, true, and free, in the dawning future.

It will be seen, from what I have said, that I consider the Ancien Regime to begin in the seventeenth century. I should date its commencement - as far as that of anything so vague, unsystematic, indeed anarchic, can be defined - from the end of the Thirty Years' War, and the peace of Westphalia in 1648.

For by that time the mighty spiritual struggles and fierce religious animosities of the preceding century had worn themselves out. And, as always happens, to a period of earnest excitement had succeeded one of weariness, disgust, half-unbelief in the many questions for which so much blood had been shed. No man had come out of the battle with altogether clean hands; some not without changing sides more than once. The war had ended as one, not of nations, not even of zealots, but of mercenaries. The body of Europe had been pulled in pieces between them all; and the poor soul thereof - as was to be expected - had fled out through the gaping wounds. Life, mere existence, was the most pressing need. If men could - in the old prophet's words - find the life of their hand, they were content. High and low only asked to be let live. The poor asked it - slaughtered on a hundred battle-fields, burnt out of house and home: vast tracts of the centre of Europe were lying desert; the population was

Charles Kingsley

diminished for several generations. The trading classes, ruined by the long war, only asked to be let live, and make a little money. The nobility, too, only asked to be let live. They had lost, in the long struggle, not only often lands and power, but their ablest and bravest men; and a weaker and meaner generation was left behind, to do the governing of the world. Let them live, and keep what they had. If signs of vigour still appeared in France, in the wars of Louis XIV. they were feverish, factitious, temporary - soon, as the event proved, to droop into the general exhaustion. If wars were still to be waged they were to be wars of succession, wars of diplomacy; not wars of principle, waged for the mightiest invisible interests of man. The exhaustion was general; and to it we must attribute alike the changes and the conservatism of the Ancien Regime. To it is owing that growth of a centralising despotism, and of arbitrary regal power, which M. de Tocqueville has set forth in a book which I shall have occasion often to quote. To it is owing, too, that longing, which seems to us childish, after ancient forms, etiquettes, dignities, court costumes, formalities diplomatic, legal, ecclesiastical. Men clung to them as to keepsakes of the past - revered relics of more intelligible and better-ordered times. If the spirit had been beaten out of them in a century of battle, that was all the more reason for keeping up the letter. They had had a meaning once, a life once; perhaps there was a little life left in them still; perhaps the dry bones would clothe themselves with flesh once more, and stand upon their feet. At least it was useful that the common people should so believe. There was good hope that the simple masses, seeing the old dignities and formalities still parading the streets, should suppose that they still contained men, and were not mere wooden figures, dressed artistically in official costume. And, on the whole, that hope was not deceived. More than a century of bitter experience was needed ere the masses discovered that their ancient rulers were like the suits of armour in the Tower of London - empty iron astride of wooden steeds, and armed with lances which every ploughboy could wrest out of their hands, and use in his own behalf.

The mistake of the masses was pardonable. For those suits of armour had once held living men; strong, brave, wise; men of an admirable temper; doing their work according to their light, not altogether well - what man does that on earth? - but well enough to make themselves necessary to, and loyally followed by, the masses whom they ruled. No one can read fairly the "Gesta Dei per Francos in Oriente," or the deeds of the French Nobility in their wars with England, or those tales - however legendary - of the mediaeval knights, which form so noble an element in German literature, without seeing, that however black were these men's occasional crimes, they were a truly noble race, the old Nobility of the Continent; a race which ruled simply because, without them, there would have been naught but anarchy and barbarism. To their chivalrous ideal they were too often, perhaps for the most part, untrue: but, partial and defective as it is, it is an ideal such as never entered into the mind of Celt or Gaul, Hun or Sclav; one which seems continuous with the spread of the Teutonic conquerors. They ruled because they did practically raise the ideal of humanity in the countries which they conquered, a whole stage higher. They ceased to rule when they were, through their own sins, caught up and surpassed in the race of progress by the classes below them.

But, even when at its best, their system of government

Charles Kingsley

had in it - like all human invention - original sin; an unnatural and unrighteous element, which was certain, sooner or later, to produce decay and ruin. The old Nobility of Europe was not a mere aristocracy. It was a caste: a race not intermarrying with the races below it. It was not a mere aristocracy. For that, for the supremacy of the best men, all societies strive, or profess to strive. And such a true aristocracy may exist independent of caste, or the hereditary principle at all. We may conceive an Utopia, governed by an aristocracy which should be really democratic; which should use, under developed forms, that method which made the mediaeval priesthood the one great democratic institution of old Christendom; bringing to the surface and utilising the talents and virtues of all classes, even to the lowest. We may conceive an aristocracy choosing out, and gladly receiving into its own ranks as equals, every youth, every maiden, who was distinguished by intellect, virtue, valour, beauty, without respect to rank or birth; and rejecting in turn, from its own ranks, each of its own children who fell below some lofty standard, and showed by weakliness, dulness, or baseness, incapacity for the post of guiding and elevating their fellow-citizens. Thus would arise a true aristocracy; a governing body of the really most worthy - the most highly organised in body and in mind - perpetually recruited from below: from which, or from any other ideal, we are yet a few thousand years distant.

But the old Ancien Regime would have shuddered, did shudder, at such a notion. The supreme class was to keep itself pure, and avoid all taint of darker blood, shutting its eyes to the fact that some of its most famous heroes had been born of such left-handed marriages as that of Robert of Normandy with the tanner's daughter of Falaise. "Some are so curious in this behalf," says quaint old Burton, writing about 1650, "as these old Romans, our modern Venetians, Dutch, and French, that if two parties dearly love, the one noble, the other ignoble, they may not, by their laws, match, though equal otherwise in years, fortunes, education, and all good affection. In Germany, except they can prove their gentility by three descents, they scorn to match with them. A nobleman must marry a noblewoman; a baron, a baron's daughter; a knight, a knight's. As slaters sort their slates, do they degrees and families."

And doubtless this theory - like all which have held their ground for many centuries - at first represented a fact. These castes were, at first, actually superior to the peoples over whom they ruled. I cannot, as long as my eyes are open, yield to the modern theory of the equality - indeed of the non-existence - of races. Holding, as I do, the primaeval unity of the human race, I see in that race the same inclination to sport into fresh varieties, the same competition of species between those varieties, which Mr. Darwin has pointed out among plants and mere animals. A distinguished man arises; from him a distinguished family; from it a distinguished tribe, stronger, cunninger than those around. It asserts its supremacy over its neighbours at first exactly as a plant or animal would do, by destroying, and, where possible, eating them; next, having grown more prudent, by enslaving them; next, having gained a little morality in addition to its prudence, by civilising them, raising them more or less toward its own standard. And thus, in every land, civilisation and national life has arisen out of the patriarchal state; and the Eastern scheik, with his wives, free and slave, and his hundreds of fighting men born in his house, is the type of all primaeval rulers. He is the best man of his horde - in every sense of the word best; and whether he have a right to rule them or not, they consider that he has, and are the better men for his guidance.

Whether this ought to have been the history of primaeval civilisation, is a question not to be determined here. That it is the history thereof, is surely patent to anyone who will imagine to himself what must have been. In the first place, the strongest and cunningest savage must have had the chance of producing children more strong and cunning than the average; he would have - the strongest savage has still - the power of obtaining a wife, or wives, superior in beauty and in household skill, which involves superiority of intellect; and therefore his children would - some of them at least - be superior to the average, both from the father's and the mother's capacities. They again would marry select wives; and their children again would do the same; till, in a very few generations, a family would have established itself, considerably superior to the rest of the tribe in body and mind, and become assuredly its ruling race.

Again, if one of that race invented a new weapon, a new mode of tillage, or aught else which gave him power, that would add to the superiority of his whole family. For the invention would be jealously kept among them as a mystery, a hereditary secret. To this simple cause, surely, is to be referred the system of hereditary caste occupations, whether in Egypt or Hindoostan. To this, too, the fact that alike in Greek and in Teutonic legend the chief so often appears, not merely as the best warrior and best minstrel, but as the best smith, armourer, and handicraftsman of his tribe.

If, however, the inventor happened to be a low-born genius, its advantages would still accrue to the ruling race. For nothing could be more natural or more easy - as more than one legend intimates - than that the king should extort the new secret from his subject, and then put him to death to prevent any further publicity.

Two great inventive geniuses we may see dimly through the abysses of the past, both of whom must have become in their time great chiefs, founders of mighty aristocracies - it may be, worshipped after their death as gods.

The first, who seems to have existed after the age in which the black race colonised Australia, must have been surely a man worthy to hold rank with our Brindleys, Watts, and Stephensons. For he invented (and mind, one man must have invented the thing first, and by the very nature of it, invented it all at once) an instrument so singular, unexpected, unlike anything to be seen in nature, that I wonder it has not been called, like the plough, the olive, or the vine, a gift of the immortal gods: and yet an instrument so simple, so easy, and so perfect, that it spread over all races in Europe and America, and no substitute could be found for it till the latter part of the fifteenth century. Yes, a great genius was he, and the consequent founder of a great aristocracy and conquering race, who first invented for himself and his children after him a - bow and arrow.

The next - whether before or after the first in time, it suits me to speak of him in second place - was the man who was the potential ancestor of the whole Ritterschaft, Chivalry, and knightly caste of Europe; the man who first, finding a foal upon the steppe, deserted by its dam, brought it home, and reared it; and then bethought him of the happy notion of making it draw - presumably by its tail - a fashion which endured long in Ireland, and had to be forbidden by law, I think as late as the sixteenth century. A great aristocrat must that man have become. A greater still he who first substituted the bit for the halter. A greater still he who first thought of wheels. A greater still he who conceived the yoke and pole for bearing up his chariot; for that same yoke, and pole, and chariot, became the peculiar instrument of conquerors like him who mightily oppressed the children of Israel, for he had nine hundred chariots of iron. Egyptians, Syrians, Assyrians, Greeks, Romans - none of them improved on the form of the conquering biga, till it was given up by a race who preferred a pair of shafts to their carts, and who had learnt to ride instead of drive. A great aristocrat, again, must he have been among those latter races who first conceived the notion of getting on his horse's back, accommodating his motions to the beast's, and becoming a centaur, half-man, half-horse. That invention must have tended, in the first instance, as surely toward democracy as did the invention of firearms. A tribe of riders must have been always, more or less, equal and free. Equal because a man on a horse would feel himself a man indeed; because the art of riding called out an independence, a self-help, a skill, a consciousness of power, a personal pride and vanity, which would defy slavery. Free, because a tribe of riders might be defeated, exterminated, but never enchained. They could never become gleboe adscripti, bound to the soil, as long as they could take horse and saddle, and away. History gives us more than one glimpse of such tribes - the scourge and terror of the non-riding races with whom they came in contact. Some, doubtless, remember how in the wars between

Alfred and the Danes, "the army" (the Scandinavian invaders) again and again horse themselves, steal away by night from the Saxon infantry, and ride over the land (whether in England or in France), "doing unspeakable evil." To that special instinct of horsemanship, which still distinguishes their descendants, we may attribute mainly the Scandinavian settlement of the north and east of England. Some, too, may recollect the sketch of the primeval Hun, as he first appeared to the astonished and disgusted old Roman soldier Ammianus Marcellinus; the visages "more like cakes than faces;" the "figures like those which are hewn out with an axe on the poles at bridge-ends;" the rat-skin coats, which they wore till they rotted off their limbs; their steaks of meat cooked between the saddle and the thigh; the little horses on which "they eat and drink, buy and sell, and sleep lying forward along his narrow neck, and indulging in every variety of dream." And over and above, and more important politically, the common councils "held on horseback, under the authority of no king, but content with the irregular government of nobles, under whose leading they force their way through all obstacles." A race - like those Cossacks who are probably their lineal descendants - to be feared, to be hired, to be petted, but not to be conquered.

Instances nearer home of free equestrian races we have in our own English borderers, among whom (as Mr. Froude says) the farmers and their farm-servants had but to snatch their arms and spring into their saddles and they became at once the Northern Horse, famed as the finest light cavalry in the world. And equal to them - superior even, if we recollect that they preserved their country's freedom for centuries against the superior force of England - were those troops of Scots who, century after century, swept across the border on their little garrons, their bag of oatmeal hanging by the saddle, with the iron griddle whereon to bake it; careless of weather and of danger; men too swift to be exterminated, too independent to be enslaved.

But if horsemanship had, in these cases, a levelling tendency it would have the very opposite when a riding tribe conquered a non-riding one. The conquerors would, as much as possible, keep the art and mystery of horsemanship hereditary among themselves, and become a Ritterschaft or chivalrous caste. And they would be able to do so: because the conquered race would not care or dare to learn the new and dangerous art. There are persons, even in England, who can never learn to ride. There are whole populations in Europe, even now, when races have become almost indistinguishably mixed, who seem unable to learn. And this must have been still more the case when the races were more strongly separated in blood and habits. So the Teutonic chief, with his gesitha, comites, or select band of knights, who had received from him, as Tacitus has it, the war-horse and the lance, established himself as the natural ruler - and oppressor - of the non-riding populations; first over the aborigines of Germany proper, tribes who seem to have been enslaved, and their names lost, before the time of Tacitus; and then over the non-riding Romans and Gauls to the South and West, and the Wendish and Sclavonic tribes to the East. Very few in numbers, but mighty in their unequalled capacity of body and mind, and in their terrible horsemanship, the Teutonic Ritterschaft literally rode roughshod over the old world; never checked, but when they came in contact with the free-riding hordes of the Eastern steppes; and so established an equestrian caste, of which the [Greek text] of Athens and the Equites of Rome had been only hints ending in failure and absorption.

Of that equestrian caste the symbol was the horse. The favourite, and therefore the chosen sacrifice of Odin, their ancestor and God, the horse's flesh was eaten at the sacrificial meal; the horse's head, hung on the ash in Odin's wood, gave forth oracular responses. As Christianity came in, and the eating of horse-flesh was forbidden as impiety by the Church, while his oracles dwindled down to such as that which Falada's dead head gives to the goose-girl in the German tale, the magic power of the horse figured only in ballads and legends: but his real power remained.

The art of riding became an hereditary and exclusive science - at last a pedantry, hampered by absurd etiquettes, and worse than useless traditions; but the power and right to ride remained on the whole the mark of the dominant caste. Terribly did they often abuse that special power. The faculty of making a horse carry him no more makes a man a good man, than the faculties of making money, making speeches, making books, or making a noise about public abuses. And of all ruffians, the worst, if history is to be trusted, is the ruffian on a horse; to whose brutality of mind is superadded the brute power of his beast. A ruffian on a horse - what is there that he will not ride over, and ride on, careless and proud of his own shame? When the ancient chivalry of France descended to that level, or rather delegated their functions to mercenaries of that level - when the knightly hosts who fought before Jerusalem allowed themselves to be superseded by the dragoons and dragonnades of Louis XIV. - then the end of the French chivalry was at hand, and came. But centuries before that shameful fall there had come in with Christianity the new thought, that domination meant responsibility; that responsibility demanded virtue. The words which denoted rank, came to denote likewise high moral excellencies. The nobilis, or man who was known, and therefore subject to public opinion, was bound to behave nobly. The gentleman - gentile-man - who respected his own gens, or family and pedigree, was bound to be gentle. The courtier, who had picked up at court some touch of Roman civilisation from Roman ecclesiastics, was bound to be courteous. He who held an "honour" or "edel" of land was bound to be honourable; and he who held a "weorthig," or worthy, thereof, was bound himself to be worthy. In like wise, he who had the right to ride a horse, was expected to be chivalrous in all matters befitting the hereditary ruler, who owed a sacred debt to a long line of forefathers, as well as to the state in which he dwelt; all dignity, courtesy, purity, self-restraint, devotion - such as they were understood in those rough days - centred themselves round the idea of the rider as the attributes of the man whose supposed duty, as well as his supposed right, was to govern his fellow-men, by example, as well as by law and force; - attributes which gathered themselves up into that one word - Chivalry: an idea, which, perfect or imperfect, God forbid that mankind should ever forget, till it has become the possession - as it is the God-given right - of the poorest slave that ever trudged on foot; and every collier-lad shall have become - as some of those Barnsley men proved but the other day they had become already:

A very gentle perfect knight,

Very unfaithful was chivalry to its ideal - as all men are to all ideals. But bear in mind, that if the horse was the symbol of the ruling caste, it was not at first its only strength. Unless that caste had had at first spiritual, as well as physical force on its side, it would have been soon destroyed - nay, it would have destroyed itself - by internecine civil war. And we must believe that those Franks, Goths, Lombards, and Burgunds, who in the early Middle Age leaped on the backs (to use Mr. Carlyle's expression) of the Roman nations, were actually, in all senses of the word, better men than those whom they conquered. We must believe it from reason; for if not, how could they, numerically few, have held for a year, much more for centuries, against millions, their dangerous elevation? We must believe it, unless we take Tacitus's "Germania," which I absolutely refuse to do, for a romance. We must believe that they were better than the Romanised nations whom they conquered, because the writers of those nations, Augustine, Salvian, and Sidonius Apollinaris, for example, say that they were such, and give proof thereof. Not good men according to our higher standard - far from it; though Sidonius's picture of Theodoric, the East Goth, in his palace of Narbonne, is the picture of an eminently good and wise ruler. But not good, I say, as a rule - the Franks, alas! often very bad men: but still better, wiser, abler, than those whom they ruled. We must believe too, that they were better, in every sense of the word, than those tribes on their eastern frontier, whom they conquered in after centuries, unless we discredit (which we have no reason to do) the accounts which the Roman and Greek writers give of the horrible savagery of those tribes.

So it was in later centuries. One cannot read fairly the history of the Middle Ages without seeing that the robber knight of Germany or of France, who figures so much in modern novels, must have been the exception, and not the rule: that an aristocracy which lived by the saddle would have as little chance of perpetuating itself, as a priesthood composed of hypocrites and profligates; that the mediaeval Nobility has been as much slandered as the mediaeval Church; and the exceptions taken - as more salient and exciting - for the average: that side by side with ruffians like Gaston de Foix hundreds of honest gentlemen were trying to do their duty to the best of their light, and were raising, and not depressing, the masses below them - one very important item in that duty being, the doing the whole fighting of the country at their own expense, instead of leaving it to a standing army of mercenaries, at the beck and call of a despot; and that, as M. de Tocqueville says: "In feudal times, the Nobility were regarded pretty much as the government is regarded in our own; the burdens they imposed were endured in consequence of the security they afforded. The nobles had many irksome privileges; they possessed many onerous rights: but they maintained public order, they administered justice, they caused the law to be executed, they came to the relief of the weak, they conducted the business of the community. In proportion as they ceased to do these things, the burden of their privileges appeared more oppressive, and their existence became an anomaly in proportion as they ceased to do these things." And the Ancien Regime may be defined as the period in which they ceased to do these things - in which they began to play the idlers, and expected to take their old wages without doing their old work.

But in any case, government by a ruling caste, whether of the patriarchal or of the feudal kind, is no ideal or permanent state of society. So far from it, it is but the first or second step out of primeval savagery. For the more a ruling race becomes conscious of its own duty, and not merely of its own power - the more it learns to regard its peculiar gifts as entrusted to it for the good of men - so much the more earnestly will it labour to raise the masses below to its own level, by imparting to them its own light; and so will it continually tend to abolish itself, by producing a general equality, moral and intellectual; and fulfil that law of self-sacrifice which is the beginning and the end of all virtue.

A race of noblest men and women, trying to make all below them as noble as themselves - that is at least a fair ideal, tending toward, though it has not reached, the highest ideal of all.

But suppose that the very opposite tendency - inherent in the heart of every child of man - should conquer. Suppose the ruling caste no longer the physical, intellectual, and moral superiors of the mass, but their equals. Suppose them - shameful, but not without example - actually sunk to be their inferiors. And that such a fall did come - nay, that it must have come - is matter of history. And its cause, like all social causes, was not a political nor a physical, but a moral cause. The profligacy of the French and Italian aristocracies, in the sixteenth century, avenged itself on them by a curse (derived from the newly-discovered America) from which they never recovered. The Spanish aristocracy suffered, I doubt not very severely. The English and German, owing to the superior homeliness and purity of ruling their lives, hardly at all. But the continental caste, instead of recruiting their tainted blood by healthy blood from below, did all, under pretence of keeping it pure, to keep it tainted by continual intermarriage; and paid, in increasing weakness of body and mind, the penalty of their exclusive pride. It is impossible for anyone who reads the French memoirs of the sixteenth and seventeenth centuries, not to perceive, if he be wise, that the aristocracy therein depicted was ripe for ruin - yea, already ruined - under any form of government whatsoever, independent of all political changes. Indeed, many of the political changes were not the causes but the effects of the demoralisation of the noblesse. Historians will tell you how, as early as the beginning of the seventeenth century, Henry IV. complained that the nobles were quitting their country districts; how succeeding kings and statesmen, notably Richelieu and Louis XIV., tempted the noblesse up to Paris, that they might become mere courtiers, instead of powerful country gentlemen; how those who remained behind were only the poor hobereaux, little hobby-hawks among the gentry, who considered it degradation to help in governing the parish, as their forefathers had governed it, and lived shabbily in their chateaux, grinding the last farthing out of their tenants, that they might spend it in town during the winter. No wonder that with such an aristocracy, who had renounced that very duty of governing the country, for which alone they and their forefathers had existed, there arose government by intendants and sub-delegates, and all the other evils of administrative centralisation, which M. de Tocqueville anatomises and deplores. But what was the cause of the curse? Their moral degradation. What drew them up to Paris save vanity and profligacy? What kept them from intermarrying with the middle class save pride? What made them give up the office of governors save idleness? And if vanity, profligacy, pride, and idleness be not injustices and moral vices, what are?

The race of heroic knights and nobles who fought under the walls of Jerusalem - who wrestled, and not in vain, for centuries with the equally heroic English, in defence of their native soil - who had set to all Europe the example of all knightly virtues, had rotted down to this; their only virtue left, as Mr. Carlyle says, being - a perfect readiness to fight duels.

Every Intendant, chosen by the Comptroller-General out of the lower-born members of the Council of State; a needy young plebeian with his fortune to make, and a stranger to the province, was, in spite of his greed, ambition, chicane, arbitrary tyranny, a better man - abler, more energetic, and often, to judge from the pages of De Tocqueville, with far more sympathy and mercy for the wretched peasantry - than was the count or marquis in the chateau above, who looked down on him as a roturier; and let him nevertheless become first his deputy, and then his master.

Understand me - I am not speaking against the hereditary principle of the Ancien Regime, but against its caste principle - two widely different elements, continually confounded nowadays.

The hereditary principle is good, because it is founded on fact and nature. If men's minds come into the world blank sheets of paper - which I much doubt - every other part and faculty of them comes in stamped with hereditary tendencies and peculiarities. There are such things as transmitted capabilities for good and for evil; and as surely as the offspring of a good horse or dog is likely to be good, so is the offspring of a good man, and still more of a good woman. If the parents have any special ability, their children will probably inherit it, at least in part; and over and above, will have it

Charles Kingsley

developed in them by an education worthy of their parents and themselves. If man were - what he is not - a healthy and normal species, a permanent hereditary caste might go on intermarrying, and so perpetuate itself. But the same moral reason which would make such a caste dangerous - indeed, fatal to the liberty and development of mankind, makes it happily impossible. Crimes and follies are certain, after a few generations, to weaken the powers of any human caste; and unless it supplements its own weakness by mingling again with the common stock of humanity, it must sink under that weakness, as the ancient noblesse sank by its own vice. Of course there were exceptions. The French Revolution brought those exceptions out into strong light; and like every day of judgment, divided between the good and the evil. But it lies not in exceptions to save a caste, or an institution; and a few Richelieus, Liancourts, Rochefoucaulds, Noailles, Lafayettes were but the storks among the cranes involved in the wholesale doom due not to each individual, but to a system and a class.

Profligacy, pride, idleness - these are the vices which we have to lay to the charge of the Teutonic Nobility of the Ancien Regime in France especially; and (though in a less degree perhaps) over the whole continent of Europe. But below them, and perhaps the cause of them all, lay another and deeper vice - godlessness - atheism.

I do not mean merely want of religion, doctrinal unbelief. I mean want of belief in duty, in responsibility. Want of belief that there was a living God governing the universe, who had set them their work, and would judge them according to their work. And therefore, want of belief, yea, utter unconsciousness, that they were set in their places to make the masses below them better men; to impart to them their own civilisation, to raise them to their own level. They would have shrunk from that which I just now defined as the true duty of an aristocracy, just because it would have seemed to them madness to abolish themselves. But the process of abolition went on, nevertheless, only now from without instead of from within. So it must always be, in such a case. If a ruling class will not try to raise the masses to their own level, the masses will try to drag them down to theirs. That sense of justice which allowed privileges, when they were as strictly official privileges as the salary of a judge, or the immunity of a member of the House of Commons; when they were earned, as in the Middle Age, by severe education, earnest labour, and life and death responsibility in peace and war, will demand the abolition of those privileges, when no work is done in return for them, with a voice which must be heard, for it is the voice of truth and justice.

But with that righteous voice will mingle another, most wicked, and yet, alas! most flattering to poor humanity - the voice of envy, simple and undisguised; of envy, which moralists hold to be one of the basest of human passions; which can never be justified, however hateful or unworthy be the envied man. And when a whole people, or even a majority thereof, shall be possessed by that, what is there that they will not do?

Some are surprised and puzzled when they find, in the French Revolution of 1793, the noblest and the foulest characters labouring in concert, and side by side - often, too, paradoxical as it may seem, united in the same personage. The explanation is simple. Justice inspired the one; the other was the child of simple envy. But this passion of envy, if it becomes permanent and popular, may avenge itself, like all other sins. A nation may say to itself, "Provided we have no superiors to fall our pride, we are content. Liberty is a slight matter, provided we have equality. Let us be slaves, provided we are all slaves alike." It may destroy every standard of humanity above its own mean average; it may forget that the old ruling class, in spite of all its defects and crimes, did at least pretend to represent something higher than man's necessary wants, plus the greed of amassing money; never meeting (at least in the country districts) any one wiser or more refined than an official or a priest drawn from the peasant class, it may lose the belief that any standard higher than that is needed; and, all but forgetting the very existence of civilisation, sink contented into a dead level of intellectual mediocrity and moral barbarism, crying, "Let us eat and drink, for to-morrow we die."

A nation in such a temper will surely be taken at its word. Where the carcase is, there the eagles will be gathered together; and there will not be wanting to such nations - as there were not wanting in old Greece and Rome - despots who will give them all they want, and more, and say to them: "Yes, you shall eat and drink; and yet you shall not die. For I, while I take care of your mortal bodies, will see that care is taken of your immortal souls."

For there are those who have discovered, with the kings of the Holy Alliance, that infidelity and scepticism are political mistakes, not so much because they promote vice, as because they promote (or are supposed to promote) free thought; who see that religion (no matter of what quality) is a most valuable assistant to the duties of a minister of police. They will quote in their own behalf Montesquieu's opinion that religion is a column necessary to sustain the social edifice; they will quote, too, that sound and true saying of De Tocqueville's: {1} "If the first American who might be met, either in his own country, or abroad, were to be stopped and asked whether he considered religion useful to the stability of the laws and the good order of society, he would answer, without hesitation, that no civilised society, but more especially none in a state of freedom, can exist without religion. Respect for religion is, in his eyes, the greatest guarantee of the stability of the State, and of the safety of the community. Those who are ignorant of the science of government, know that fact at least."

M. de Tocqueville, when he wrote these words, was lamenting that in France, "freedom was forsaken;" "a thing for which it is said that no one any longer cares in France." He did not, it seems to me, perceive that, as in America the best guarantee of freedom is the reverence for a religion or religions, which are free themselves, and which teach men to be free; so in other countries the best guarantee of slavery is, reverence for religions which are not free, and which teach men to be slaves.

But what M. de Tocqueville did not see, there are others who will see; who will say: "If religion be the pillar of political and social order, there is an order which is best supported by a religion which is adverse to free thought, free speech, free conscience, free communion between man and God. The more enervating the superstition, the more exacting and tyrannous its priesthood, the more it will do our work, if we help it to do its own. If it permit us to enslave the body, we will permit it to enslave the soul."

And so may be inaugurated a period of that organised anarchy of which the poet says:

It is not life, but death, when nothing stirs.

LECTURE II - CENTRALISATION

The degradation of the European nobility caused, of course, the increase of the kingly power, and opened the way to central despotisms. The bourgeoisie, the commercial middle class, whatever were its virtues, its value, its real courage, were never able to stand alone against the kings. Their capital, being invested in trade, was necessarily subject to such sudden dangers from war, political change, bad seasons, and so forth, that its holders, however individually brave, were timid as a class. They could never hold out on strike against the governments, and had to submit to the powers that were, whatever they were, under penalty of ruin.

But on the Continent, and especially in France and Germany, unable to strengthen itself by intermarriage with the noblesse, they retained that timidity which is the fruit of the insecurity of trade; and had to submit to a more and more centralised despotism, and grow up as they could, in the face of exasperating hindrances to wealth, to education, to the possession, in many parts of France, of large landed estates; leaving the noblesse to decay in isolated uselessness and weakness, and in many cases debt and poverty.

The system - or rather anarchy - according to which France was governed during this transitional period, may be read in that work of M. de Tocqueville's which

I have already quoted, and which is accessible to all classes, through Mr. H. Reeve's excellent translation. Every student of history is, of course, well acquainted with that book. But as there is reason to fear, from language which is becoming once more too common, both in speech and writing, that the general public either do not know it, or have not understood it, I shall take the liberty of quoting from it somewhat largely. I am justified in so doing by the fact that M. de Tocqueville's book is founded on researches into the French Archives, which have been made (as far as I am aware) only by him; and contains innumerable significant facts, which are to be found (as far as I am aware) in no other accessible work.

The French people - says M. de Tocqueville - made, in 1789, the greatest effort which was ever made by any nation to cut, so to speak, their destiny in halves, and to separate by an abyss that which they had heretofore been, from that which they sought to become hereafter. But he had long thought that they had succeeded in this singular attempt much less than was supposed abroad; and less than they had at first supposed themselves. He was convinced that they had unconsciously retained, from the former state of society, most of the sentiments, the habits, and even the opinions, by means of which they had effected the destruction of that state of things; and that, without intending it, they had used its remains to rebuild the edifice of modern society. This is his thesis, and this he proves, it seems to me, incontestably by documentary evidence. Not only does he find habits which we suppose - or supposed till lately - to have died with the eighteenth century, still living and working, at least in France, in the nineteenth, but the new opinions which we look on usually as the special children of the nineteenth century, he shows to have been born in the eighteenth. France, he considers, is still at heart what the Ancien Regime made her.

He shows that the hatred of the ruling caste, the intense determination to gain and keep equality, even at the expense of liberty, had been long growing up, under those influences of which I spoke in my first lecture.

He shows, moreover, that the acquiescence in a centralised administration; the expectation that the government should do everything for the people, and nothing for themselves; the consequent loss of local liberties, local peculiarities; the helplessness of the towns and the parishes: and all which issued in making Paris France, and subjecting the whole of a vast country to the arbitrary dictates of a knot of despots in the capital, was not the fruit of the Revolution, but of the Ancien Regime which preceded it; and that Robespierre and his "Comite de Salut Public," and commissioners sent forth to the four winds of heaven in bonnet rouge and carmagnole complete, to build up and pull down, according to their wicked will, were only handling, somewhat more roughly, the same wires which had been handled for several generations by the Comptroller-General and Council of State, with their provincial intendants.

"Do you know," said Law to the Marquis d'Argenson, "that this kingdom of France is governed by thirty intendants? You have neither parliament, nor estates, nor governors. It is upon thirty masters of request, despatched into the provinces, that their evil or their good, their fertility or their sterility, entirely depend."

To do everything for the people, and let them do

nothing for themselves - this was the Ancien Regime. To be more wise and more loving than Almighty God, who certainly does not do everything for the sons of men, but forces them to labour for themselves by bitter need, and after a most Spartan mode of education; who allows them to burn their hands as often as they are foolish enough to put them into the fire; and to be filled with the fruits of their own folly, even though the folly be one of necessary ignorance; treating them with that seeming neglect which is after all the most provident care, because by it alone can men be trained to experience, self-help, science, true humanity; and so become not tolerably harmless dolls, but men and women worthy of the name; with

> The reason firm, the temperate will,
> Endurance, foresight, strength, and skill;
> The perfect spirit, nobly planned
> To cheer, to counsel, and command.

Such seems to be the education and government appointed for man by the voluntatem Dei in rebus revelatum, and the education, therefore, which the man of science will accept and carry out. But the men of the Ancien Regime - in as far as it was a Regime at all - tried to be wiser than the Almighty. Why not? They were not the first, nor will be the last, by many who have made the same attempt. So this Council of State settled arbitrarily, not only taxes, and militia, and roads, but anything and everything. Its members meddled, with their whole hearts and minds. They tried to teach agriculture by schools and pamphlets and prizes; they sent out plans for every public work. A town could not establish an octroi, levy a rate, mortgage, sell, sue, farm, or administer their property, without an order in council. The Government ordered public rejoicings, saw to the firing of salutes, and illuminating of houses - in one case mentioned by M. de Tocqueville, they fined a member of the burgher guard for absenting himself from a Te Deum. All self-government was gone. A country parish was, says Turgot, nothing but "an assemblage of cabins, and of inhabitants as passive as the cabins they dwelt in." Without an order of council, the parish could not mend the steeple after a storm, or repair the parsonage gable. If they grumbled at the intendant, he threw some of the chief persons into prison, and made the parish pay the expenses of the horse patrol, which formed the arbitrary police of France. Everywhere was meddling. There were reports on statistics - circumstantial, inaccurate, and useless - as statistics are too often wont to be. Sometimes, when the people were starving, the Government sent down charitable donations to certain parishes, on condition that the inhabitants should raise a sum on their part. When the sum offered was sufficient, the Comptroller-General wrote on the margin, when he returned the report to the intendant, "Good - express satisfaction." If it was more than sufficient, he wrote, "Good - express satisfaction and sensibility." There is nothing new under the sun. In 1761, the Government, jealous enough of newspapers, determined to start one for itself, and for that purpose took under its tutelage the Gazette de France. So the public newsmongers were of course to be the provincial intendants, and their sub-newsmongers, of course, the sub-delegates.

But alas! the poor sub-delegates seem to have found either very little news, or very little which it was politic to publish. One reports that a smuggler of salt has been hung, and has displayed great courage; another that a woman in his district has had three girls at a birth; another that a dreadful storm has happened, but - has done no mischief; a fourth - living in some specially favoured Utopia - declares that in spite of all his efforts he has found nothing worth recording, but that he himself will subscribe to so useful a journal, and will exhort all respectable persons to follow his example: in spite of which loyal endeavours, the journal seems to have proved a failure, to the great disgust of the king and his minister, who had of course expected to secure fine weather by nailing, like the schoolboy before a holiday, the hand of the weather-glass.

Well had it been, if the intermeddling of this bureaucracy had stopped there. But, by a process of evocation (as it was called), more and more causes, criminal as well as civil, were withdrawn from the regular tribunals, to those of the intendants and the Council. Before the intendant all the lower order of people were generally sent for trial. Bread-riots were a common cause of such trials, and M. de Tocqueville asserts that he has found sentences, delivered by the intendant, and a local council chosen by himself, by which men were condemned to the galleys, and even to death. Under such a system, under which an intendant must have felt it his interest to pretend at all risks, that all was going right, and to regard any disturbance as a dangerous exposure of himself and his chiefs - one can understand easily enough that scene which Mr. Carlyle has dramatised from Lacretelle, concerning the canaille, the masses, as we used to call them a generation since:

"A dumb generation - their voice only an inarticulate cry. Spokesman, in the king's council, in the world's forum, they have none that finds credence. At rare intervals (as now, in 1775) they will fling down their hoes, and hammers; and, to the astonishment of mankind, flock hither and thither, dangerous, aimless, get the length even of Versailles. Turgot is altering the corn trade, abrogating the absurdest corn laws; there is dearth, real, or were it even factitious, an indubitable scarcity of broad. And so, on the 2nd day of May, 1775, these waste multitudes do here, at Versailles chateau, in widespread wretchedness, in sallow faces, squalor, winged raggedness, present as in legible hieroglyphic writing their petition of grievances. The chateau-gates must be shut; but the king will appear on the balcony and speak to them. They have seen the king's face; their petition of grievances has been, if not read, looked at. In answer, two of them are hanged, on a new gallows forty feet high, and the rest driven back to their dens for a time."

Of course. What more exasperating and inexpiable insult to the ruling powers was possible than this? To persist in being needy and wretched, when a whole bureaucracy is toiling day and night to make them prosperous and happy? An insult only to be avenged in blood. Remark meanwhile, that this centralised bureaucracy was a failure; that after all the trouble taken to govern these masses, they were not governed, in the sense of being made better, and not worse. The truth is, that no centralised bureaucracy, or so-called "paternal government," yet invented on earth, has been anything but a failure, or is it like to be anything else: because it is founded on an error; because it regards and treats men as that which they are not, as things; and not as that which they are, as persons. If the bureaucracy were a mere Briareus giant, with a hundred hands, helping the weak throughout the length and breadth of the empire, the system might be at least tolerable. But what if the Government were not a Briareus with a hundred hands, but a Hydra with a hundred heads and mouths, each far more intent on helping itself than on helping the people? What if sub-delegates and other officials, holding office at the will of the intendant, had to live, and even provide against a rainy day? What if intendants, holding office at the will of the Comptroller-General, had to do more than live, and found it prudent to realise as large a fortune as possible, not only against disgrace, but against success, and the dignity fit for a new member of the Noblesse de la Robe? Would not the system, then, soon become intolerable? Would there not be evil times for the masses, till they became something more than masses?

It is an ugly name, that of "The Masses," for the great majority of human beings in a nation. He who uses it speaks of them not as human beings, but as things; and as things not bound together in one living body, but lying in a fortuitous heap. A swarm of ants is not a mass. It has a polity and a unity. Not the ants but the fir-needles and sticks, of which the ants have piled their nest, are a mass.

The term, I believe, was invented during the Ancien Regime. Whether it was or not, it expresses very accurately the life of the many in those days. No one would speak, if he wished to speak exactly, of the masses of the United States; for there every man is, or is presumed to be, a personage; with his own independence, his own activities, his own rights and duties. No one, I believe, would have talked of the masses in the old feudal times; for then each individual was someone's man, bound to his master by ties of mutual service, just or unjust, honourable or base, but still giving him a personality of duties and rights, and dividing him from his class.

Dividing, I say. The poor of the Middle Age had little sense of a common humanity. Those who owned allegiance to the lord in the next valley were not their brothers; and at their own lord's bidding, they buckled on sword and slew the next lord's men, with joyful heart and good conscience. Only now and then misery compressed them into masses; and they ran together, as sheep run together to face a dog. Some wholesale wrong made them aware that they were brothers, at least in the power of starving; and they joined in the cry which was heard, I believe, in Mecklenburg as late as 1790: "Den Edelman wille wi dodschlagen." Then, in Wat Tyler's insurrections, in Munster Anabaptisms, in Jacqueries, they proved themselves to be masses, if nothing better, striking for awhile, by the mere weight of numbers, blows terrible, though aimless - soon to be dispersed and slain in their turn by a disciplined and compact aristocracy. Yet not always dispersed, if they could find a leader; as the Polish nobles discovered to their cost in the middle of the seventeenth century. Then Bogdan the Cossack, a wild warrior, not without his sins, but having deserved well of James Sobieski and the Poles, found that the neighbouring noble's steward had taken a fancy to his windmill and his farm upon the Dnieper. He was thrown into prison on a frivolous charge, and escaped to the Tatars, leaving his wife dishonoured, his house burnt, his infant lost in the flames, his eldest son scourged for protesting against the wrong. And he returned, at the head of an army of Tatars, Socinians, Greeks, or what not, to set free the serfs, and exterminate Jesuits, Jews, and nobles, throughout Podolia, Volhynia, Red Russia; to desecrate the altars of God, and slay his servants; to destroy the nobles by lingering tortures; to strip noble ladies and maidens, and hunt them to death with the whips of his Cossacks; and after defeating the nobles in battle after battle, to inaugurate an era of misery and anarchy from which Poland never recovered.

Thus did the masses of Southern Poland discover, for one generation at least, that they were not many things, but one thing; a class, capable of brotherhood and unity, though, alas! only of such as belongs to a pack of wolves. But such outbursts as this were rare exceptions. In general, feudalism kept the people divided, and therefore helpless. And as feudalism died out, and with it the personal self-respect and loyalty which were engendered by the old relations of master and servant, the division still remained; and the people, in France especially, became merely masses, a swarm of incoherent and disorganised things intent on the necessaries of daily bread, like mites crawling over each other in a cheese.

Out of this mass were struggling upwards perpetually, all who had a little ambition, a little scholarship, or a little money, endeavouring to become members of the middle class by obtaining a Government appointment. "A man," says M. de Tocqueville, "endowed with some education and small means, thought it not decorous to die without having been a Government officer." "Every man, according to his condition," says a contemporary writer, "wants to be something by command of the king."

It was not merely the "natural vanity" of which M. de Tocqueville accuses his countrymen, which stirred up in them this eagerness after place; for we see the same eagerness in other nations of the Continent, who cannot be accused (as wholes) of that weakness. The fact is, a Government place, or a Government decoration, cross, ribbon, or what not, is, in a country where self-government is unknown or dead, the only method, save literary fame, which is left to men in order to assert themselves either to themselves or their fellow-men.

A British or American shopkeeper or farmer asks nothing of his Government. He can, if he chooses, be elected to some local office (generally unsalaried) by the votes of his fellow-citizens. But that is his right, and adds nothing to his respectability. The test of that latter, in a country where all honest callings are equally honourable, is the amount of money he can make; and a very sound practical test that is, in a country where intellect and capital are free. Beyond that, he is what he is, and wishes to be no more, save what he can make himself. He has his rights, guaranteed by law and public opinion; and as long as he stands within them, and (as he well phrases it) behaves like a gentleman, he considers himself as good as any man; and so he is. But under the bureaucratic Regime of the Continent, if a man had not "something by command of the king," he was nothing; and something he naturally wished to be, even by means of a Government which he disliked and despised. So in France, where innumerable petty posts were regular articles of sale, anyone, it seems, who had saved a little money, found it most profitable to invest it in a beadledom of some kind - to the great detriment of the country, for he thus withdrew his capital from trade; but to his own clear gain, for he thereby purchased some immunity from public burdens, and, as it were, compounded once and for all for his taxes. The petty German princes, it seems, followed the example of France, and sold their little beadledoms likewise; but even where offices were not sold, they must be obtained by any and every means, by everyone who desired not to be as other men were, and to become Notables, as they were called in France; so he migrated from the country into the nearest town, and became a member of some small body-guild, town council, or what not, bodies which were infinite in number. In one small town M. de Tocqueville discovers thirty-six such bodies, "separated from each other by diminutive privileges, the least honourable of which was still a mark of honour." Quarrelling perpetually with each other for precedence, despising and oppressing the very menu peuple from whom they had for the most part sprung, these innumerable small bodies, instead of uniting their class, only served to split it up more and more; and when the Revolution broke them up, once and for all, with all other privileges whatsoever, no bond of union was left; and each man stood alone, proud of his "individuality" - his complete social isolation; till he discovered that, in ridding himself of superiors, he had rid himself also of fellows; fulfilling, every man in his own person, the old fable of the bundle of sticks; and had to submit, under the Consulate and the Empire, to a tyranny to which the Ancien Regime was freedom itself.

For, in France at least, the Ancien Regime was no tyranny. The middle and upper classes had individual liberty - it may be, only too much; the liberty of disobeying a Government which they did not respect. "However submissive the French may have been before the Revolution to the will of the king, one sort of obedience was altogether unknown to them. They knew not what it was to bow before an illegitimate and contested power - a power but little honoured, frequently despised, but willingly endured because it may be serviceable, or because it may hurt. To that degrading form of servitude they were ever strangers. The king inspired them with feelings . . . which have become incomprehensible to this generation . . . They loved him with the affection due to a father; they revered him with the respect due to God. In submitting to the most arbitrary of his commands, they yielded less to compulsion than to loyalty; and thus they frequently preserved great freedom of mind, even in the most complete dependence. This liberty, irregular, intermittent," says M. de Tocqueville, "helped to form those vigorous characters, those proud and daring spirits, which were to make the French Revolution at once the object of the admiration and the terror of succeeding generations."

This liberty - too much akin to anarchy, in which indeed it issued for awhile - seems to have asserted itself in continual petty resistance to officials whom they did not respect, and who, in their turn, were more than a little afraid of the very men out of whose ranks they had sprung.

The French Government - one may say, every Government on the Continent in those days - had the special weakness of all bureaucracies; namely, that want of moral force which compels them to fall back at last on physical force, and transforms the ruler into a bully, and the soldier into a policeman and a gaoler. A Government of parvenus, uncertain of its own position, will be continually trying to assert itself to itself, by vexatious intermeddling and intruding pretensions; and then, when it meets with the resistance of free and rational spirits, will either recoil in awkward cowardice, or fly into a passion, and appeal to the halter and the sword. Such a Government can never take itself for granted, because it knows that it is not taken for granted by the people. It never can possess the quiet assurance, the courteous dignity, without swagger, yet without hesitation, which belongs to hereditary legislators; by which term is to be understood, not merely kings, not merely noblemen, but every citizen of a free nation, however democratic, who has received from his forefathers the right, the duty, and the example of self-government.

Such was the political and social state of the Ancien Regime, not only in France, but if we are to trust (as we must trust) M. de Tocqueville, in almost every nation in Europe, except Britain.

And as for its moral state. We must look for that - if we have need, which happily all have not - in its lighter literature.

I shall not trouble you with criticisms on French memoirs - of which those of Madame de Sevigne are on the whole, the most painful (as witness her comments on the Marquise de Brinvilliers's execution), because written by a woman better and more human than ordinary. Nor with "Menagiana," or other 'ana's - as vain and artificial as they are often foul; nor with novels and poems, long since deservedly forgotten. On the first perusal of this lighter literature, you will be charmed with the ease, grace, lightness with which everything is said. On the second, you will be some-what cured of your admiration, as you perceive how little there is to say. The head proves to be nothing but a cunning mask, with no brains inside. Especially is this true of a book, which I must beg those who have read it already, to recollect. To read it I recommend no human being. We may consider it, as it was considered in its time, the typical novel of the Ancien Regime. A picture of Spanish society, written by a Frenchman, it was held to be - and doubtless with reason - a picture of the whole European world. Its French editor (of 1836) calls it a grande epopee; "one of the most prodigious efforts of intelligence, exhausting all forms of humanity" - in fact, a second Shakespeare, according to the lights of the year 1715. I mean, of course, "Gil Blas." So picturesque is the book, that it has furnished inexhaustible motifs to the draughtsman. So excellent is its workmanship, that the enthusiastic editor of 1836 tells us - and doubtless he knows best - that it is the classic model of the French tongue; and that, as Le Sage "had embraced all that belonged to man in his composition, he dared to prescribe to himself to embrace the whole French language in his work." It has been the parent of a whole school of literature - the Bible of tens of thousands, with admiring commentators in plenty; on whose souls may God have mercy!

And no wonder. The book has a solid value, and will always have, not merely from its perfect art (according to its own measure and intention), but from its perfect truthfulness. It is the Ancien Regime itself. It set forth to the men thereof, themselves, without veil or cowardly reticence of any kind; and inasmuch as every man loves himself, the Ancien Regime loved "Gil Blas," and said, "The problem of humanity is solved at last." But, ye long-suffering powers of heaven, what a solution! It is beside the matter to call the book ungodly, immoral, base. Le Sage would have answered: "Of course it is; for so is the world of which it is a picture." No; the most notable thing about the book is its intense stupidity; its dreariness, barrenness, shallowness, ignorance of the human heart, want of any human interest. If it be an epos, the actors in it are not men and women, but ferrets - with here and there, of course, a stray rabbit, on whose brains they may feed. It is the inhuman mirror of an inhuman age, in which the healthy human heart can find no more interest than in a pathological museum.

That last, indeed, "Gil Blas" is; a collection of diseased specimens. No man or woman in the book, lay or clerical, gentle or simple, as far as I can remember, do their duty in any wise, even if they recollect that they have any duty to do. Greed, chicane, hypocrisy, uselessness are the ruling laws of human society. A new book of Ecclesiastes, crying, "Vanity of vanity, all is vanity;" the "conclusion of the whole matter" being left out, and the new Ecclesiastes rendered thereby diabolic, instead of like that old one, divine. For, instead of "Fear God and keep his commandments, for that is the whole duty of main," Le Sage sends forth the new conclusion, "Take care of thyself, and feed on thy neighbours, for that is the whole duty of man." And very faithfully was his advice (easy enough to obey at all times) obeyed for nearly a century after "Gil Blas" appeared.

About the same time there appeared, by a remarkable coincidence, another work, like it the child of the Ancien Regime, and yet as opposite to it as light to darkness. If Le Sage drew men as they were, Fenelon tried at least to draw them as they might have been and still might be, were they governed by sages and by saints, according to the laws of God. "Telemaque" is an ideal - imperfect, doubtless, as all ideals must be in a world in which God's ways and thoughts are for ever higher than man's; but an ideal nevertheless. If its construction is less complete than that of "Gil Blas," it is because its aim is infinitely higher; because the form has to be subordinated, here and there, to the matter. If its political economy be imperfect, often chimerical, it is because the mind of one man must needs have been too weak to bring into shape and order the chaos, social and economic, which he saw around him. M. de Lamartine, in his brilliant little life of Fenelon, does not hesitate to trace to the influence of "Telemaque," the Utopias which produced the revolutions of 1793 and 1848. "The saintly poet was," he says, "without knowing it, the first Radical and the first communist of his century." But it is something to have preached to princes doctrines till then unknown, or at least forgotten for many a generation - free trade, peace, international arbitration, and the "carriere ouverte aux talents" for all ranks. It is something to have warned his generation of the dangerous overgrowth of the metropolis; to have prophesied, as an old Hebrew might have done, that the despotism which he saw around him would end in a violent revolution. It is something to have combined the highest Christian morality with a hearty appreciation of old Greek life; of its reverence for bodily health and prowess; its joyous and simple country society; its sacrificial feasts, dances, games; its respect for the gods; its belief that they helped, guided, inspired the sons of men. It is something to have himself believed in God; in a living God, who, both in this life and in all lives to come, rewarded the good and punished the evil by inevitable laws. It is something to have warned a young prince, in an age of doctrinal bigotry and practical atheism, that a living God still existed, and that his laws were still in force; to have shown him Tartarus crowded with the souls of wicked monarchs, while a few of kingly race rested in Elysium, and among them old pagans - Inachus, Cecrops, Erichthon, Triptolemus, and

Sesostris - rewarded for ever for having done their duty, each according to his light, to the flocks which the gods had committed to their care. It is something to have spoken to a prince, in such an age, without servility, and without etiquette, of the frailties and the dangers which beset arbitrary rulers; to have told him that royalty, "when assumed to content oneself, is a monstrous tyranny; when assumed to fulfil its duties, and to conduct an innumerable people as a father conducts his children, a crushing slavery, which demands an heroic courage and patience."

Let us honour the courtier who dared speak such truths; and still more the saintly celibate who had sufficient catholicity of mind to envelop them in old Grecian dress, and, without playing false for a moment to his own Christianity, seek in the writings of heathen sages a wider and a healthier view of humanity than was afforded by an ascetic creed.

No wonder that the appearance of "Telemaque," published in Holland without the permission of Fenelon, delighted throughout Europe that public which is always delighted with new truths, as long as it is not required to practise them. To read "Telemaque" was the right and the enjoyment of everyone. To obey it, the duty only of princes. No wonder that, on the other hand, this "Vengeance de peuples, lecon des rois," as M. de Lamartine calls it, was taken for the bitterest satire by Louis XIV., and completed the disgrace of one who had dared to teach the future king of France that he must show himself, in all things, the opposite of his grandfather. No wonder if Madame de Maintenon and the court looked on its portraits of wicked ministers and courtiers as caricatures of themselves; portraits too, which, "composed thus in the palace of Versailles, under the auspices of that confidence which the king had placed in the preceptor of his heir, seemed a domestic treason." No wonder, also, if the foolish and envious world outside was of the same opinion; and after enjoying for awhile this exposure of the great ones of the earth, left "Telemaque" as an Utopia with which private folks had no concern; and betook themselves to the easier and more practical model of "Gil Blas."

But there are solid defects in "Telemaque" - indicating corresponding defects in the author's mind - which would have, in any case, prevented its doing the good work which Fenelon desired; defects which are natural, as it seems to me, to his position as a Roman Catholic priest, however saintly and pure, however humane and liberal. The king, with him, is to be always the father of his people; which is tantamount to saying, that the people are to be always children, and in a condition of tutelage; voluntary, if possible: if not, of tutelage still. Of self-government, and education of human beings into free manhood by the exercise of self-government, free will, free thought - of this Fenelon had surely not a glimpse. A generation or two passed by, and then the peoples of Europe began to suspect that they were no longer children, but come to manhood; and determined (after the example of Britain and America) to assume the rights and duties of manhood, at whatever risk of excesses or mistakes: and then "Telemaque" was relegated - half unjustly - as the slavish and childish dream of a past age, into the schoolroom, where it still remains.

But there is a defect in "Telemaque" which is perhaps deeper still. No woman in it exercises influence over man, except for evil. Minerva, the guiding and inspiring spirit, assumes of course, as Mentor, a male form; but her speech and thought is essentially masculine, and not feminine. Antiope is a mere lay-figure, introduced at the end of the book because Telemachus must needs be allowed to have hope of marrying someone or other. Venus plays but the same part as she does in the Tannenhauser legends of the Middle Age. Her hatred against Telemachus is an integral element of the plot. She, with the other women or nymphs of the romance, in spite of all Fenelon's mercy and courtesy towards human frailties, really rise no higher than the witches of the Malleus Maleficanum. Woman - as the old monk held who derived femina from fe, faith, and minus, less, because women have less faith than men - is, in "Telemaque," whenever she thinks or acts, the temptress, the enchantress; the victim (according to a very ancient calumny) of passions more violent, often more lawless, than man's.

Such a conception of women must make "Telemaque," to the end of time, useless as a wholesome book of education. It must have crippled its influence, especially in France, in its own time. For there, for good and for evil, woman was asserting more and more her power, and her right to power, over the mind and heart of man. Rising from the long degradation of the Middle Ages, which had really respected her only when unsexed and celibate, the French woman had assumed, often lawlessly, always triumphantly, her just freedom; her true place as the equal, the coadjutor, the counsellor of man. Of all problems connected with the education of a young prince, that of the influence of woman was, in the France of the Ancien Regime, the most important. And it was just that which Fenelon did not, perhaps dared not, try to touch; and which he most certainly could not have solved. Meanwhile, not only Madame de Maintenon, but women whose names it were a shame to couple with hers, must have smiled at, while they hated, the saint who attempted to dispense not only with them, but with the ideal queen who should have been the helpmeet of the ideal king.

To those who believe that the world is governed by a living God, it may seem strange, at first sight, that this moral anarchy was allowed to endure; that the avenging, and yet most purifying storm of the French Revolution, inevitable from Louis XIV.'s latter years, was not allowed to burst two generations sooner than it did. Is not the answer - that the question always is not of destroying the world, but of amending it? And that amendment must always come from within, and not from without? That men must be taught to become men, and mend their world themselves? To educate men into self-government - that is the purpose of the government of God; and some of the men of the eighteenth century did not learn that lesson. As the century rolled on, the human mind arose out of the slough in which Le Sage found it, into manifold and beautiful activity, increasing hatred of shams and lies, increasing hunger after truth and usefulness. With mistakes and confusions innumerable they worked: but still they worked; planting good seed; and when the fire of the French Revolution swept over the land, it burned up the rotten and the withered, only to let the fresh herbage spring up from underneath.

But that purifying fire was needed. If we inquire why the many attempts to reform the Ancien Regime, which the eighteenth century witnessed, were failures one and all; why Pombal failed in Portugal, Aranda in Spain, Joseph II. in Austria, Ferdinand and Caroline in

Naples - for these last, be it always remembered, began as humane and enlightened sovereigns, patronising liberal opinions, and labouring to ameliorate the condition of the poor, till they were driven by the murder of Marie Antoinette into a paroxysm of rage and terror - why, above all, Louis XVI., who attempted deeper and wiser reforms than any other sovereign, failed more disastrously than any - is not the answer this, that all these reforms would but have cleansed the outside of the cup and the platter, while they left the inside full of extortion and excess? It was not merely institutions which required to be reformed, but men and women. The spirit of "Gil Blas" had to be cast out. The deadness, selfishness, isolation of men's souls; their unbelief in great duties, great common causes, great self-sacrifices - in a word, their unbelief in God, and themselves, and mankind - all that had to be reformed; and till that was done all outward reform would but have left them, at best, in brute ease and peace, to that soulless degradation, which (as in the Byzantine empire of old, and seeming in the Chinese empire of to-day) hides the reality of barbarism under a varnish of civilisation. Men had to be awakened; to be taught to think for themselves, act for themselves, to dare and suffer side by side for their country and for their children; in a word, to arise and become men once more.

And, what is more, men had to punish - to avenge. Those are fearful words. But there is, in this God-guided universe, a law of retribution, which will find men out, whether men choose to find it out or not; a law of retribution; of vengeance inflicted justly, though not necessarily by just men. The public executioner was seldom a very estimable personage, at least under the old Regime; and those who have been the scourges of God have been, in general, mere scourges, and nothing better; smiting blindly, rashly, confusedly; confounding too often the innocent with the guilty, till they have seemed only to punish crime by crime, and replace old sins by new. But, however insoluble, however saddening that puzzle be, I must believe - as long as I believe in any God at all - that such men as Robespierre were His instruments, even in their crimes.

In the case of the French Revolution, indeed, the wickedness of certain of its leaders was part of the retribution itself. For the noblesse existed surely to make men better. It did, by certain classes, the very opposite. Therefore it was destroyed by wicked men, whom it itself had made wicked. For over and above all political, economic, social wrongs, there were wrongs personal, human, dramatic; which stirred not merely the springs of covetousness or envy, or even of a just demand for the freedom of labour and enterprise: but the very deepest springs of rage, contempt, and hate; wrongs which caused, as I believe, the horrors of the Revolution.

It is notorious how many of the men most deeply implicated in those horrors were of the artist class - by which I signify not merely painters and sculptors - as the word artist has now got, somewhat strangely, to signify, at least in England - but what the French meant by ARTISTES - producers of luxuries and amusements, play-actors, musicians, and suchlike, down to that "distracted peruke-maker with two fiery torches," who, at the storm of the Bastile, "was for burning the saltpetres of the Arsenal, had not a woman run screaming; had not a patriot, with some tincture of natural philosophy, instantly struck the wind out of him, with butt of musket on pit of stomach, overturned the barrels, and stayed the devouring element." The distracted peruke-maker may have had his wrongs - perhaps such a one as that of poor Triboulet the fool, in "Le Roi s'amuse" - and his own sound reasons for blowing down the Bastile, and the system which kept it up.

For these very ministers of luxury - then miscalled art - from the periwig-maker to the play-actor - who like them had seen the frivolity, the baseness, the profligacy, of the rulers to whose vices they pandered, whom they despised while they adored! Figaro himself may have looked up to his master the Marquis as a superior being as long as the law enabled the Marquis to send him to the Bastile by a lettre de cachet; yet Figaro may have known and seen enough to excuse him, when lettres de cachet were abolished, for handing the Marquis over to a Comite de Salut Public. Disappointed play-actors, like Collet d'Herbois; disappointed poets, like Fabre d'Olivet, were, they say, especially ferocious. Why not? Ingenious, sensitive spirits, used as lap-dogs and singing-birds by men and women whom they felt to be their own flesh and blood, they had, it may be, a juster appreciation of the actual worth of their patrons than had our own Pitt and Burke. They had played the valet: and no man was a hero to them. They had seen the nobleman expose himself before his own helots: they would try if the helot was not as good as the nobleman. The nobleman had played the mountebank: why should not the mountebank, for once, play the nobleman? The nobleman's God had been his five senses, with (to use Mr. Carlyle's phrase) the sixth sense of vanity: why should not the mountebank worship the same God, like Carriere at Nantes, and see what grace and gifts he too might obtain at that altar?

But why so cruel? Because, with many of these men, I more than suspect, there were wrongs to be avenged deeper than any wrongs done to the sixth sense of vanity. Wrongs common to them, and to a great portion of the respectable middle class, and much of the lower class: but wrongs to which they and their families, being most in contact with the noblesse, would be especially exposed; namely, wrongs to women.

Everyone who knows the literature of that time, must know what I mean: what had gone on for more than a century, it may be more than two, in France, in Italy, and - I am sorry to have to say it - Germany likewise. All historians know what I mean, and how enormous was the evil. I only wonder that they have so much overlooked that item in the causes of the Revolution. It seems to me to have been more patent and potent in the sight of men, as it surely was in the sight of Almighty God, than all the political and economic wrongs put together. They might have issued in a change of dynasty or of laws. That, issued in the blood of the offenders. Not a girl was enticed into Louis XV.'s Petit Trianon, or other den of aristocratic iniquity, but left behind her, parents nursing shame and sullen indignation, even while they fingered the ill-gotten price of their daughter's honour; and left behind also, perhaps, some unhappy boy of her own class, in whom disappointment and jealousy were transformed - and who will blame him? - into righteous indignation, and a very sword of God; all the more indignant, and all the more righteous, if education helped him to see, that the maiden's acquiescence, her pride in her own shame, was the ugliest feature in the whole crime, and the most potent reason for putting an end, however fearful, to a state of things in which such a fate was thought an honour and a gain, and not a disgrace and a ruin; in which the most gifted daughters of the lower classes had learnt to think it more noble to become - that which they became - than the wives of honest men.

If you will read fairly the literature of the Ancien Regime, whether in France or elsewhere, you will see that my facts are true. If you have human hearts in you, you will see in them, it seems to me, an explanation of many a guillotinade and fusillade, as yet explained only on the ground of madness - an hypothesis which (as we do not yet in the least understand what madness is) is no explanation at all.

An age of decay, incoherence, and makeshift, varnish and gilding upon worm-eaten furniture, and mouldering wainscot, was that same Ancien Regime. And for that very reason a picturesque age; like one of its own landscapes. A picturesque bit of uncultivated mountain, swarming with the prince's game; a picturesque old robber schloss above, now in ruins; and below, perhaps, the picturesque new schloss, with its French fountains and gardens, French nymphs of marble, and of flesh and blood likewise, which the prince has partially paid for, by selling a few hundred young men to the English to fight the Yankees. The river, too, is picturesque, for the old bridge has not been repaired since it was blown up in the Seven Years' War; and there is but a single lazy barge floating down the stream, owing to the tolls and tariffs of his Serene Highness; the village is picturesque, for the flower of the young men are at the wars, and the place is tumbling down; and the two old peasants in the foreground, with the single goat and the hamper of vine-twigs, are very picturesque likewise, for they are all in rags.

How sad to see the picturesque element eliminated, and the quiet artistic beauty of the scene destroyed; - to have steamers puffing up and down the river, and a railroad hurrying along its banks the wealth of the Old World, in exchange for the wealth of the New - or hurrying, it may be, whole regiments of free and educated citizen-soldiers, who fight, they know for what. How sad to see the alto schloss desecrated by tourists, and the neue schloss converted into a cold-water cure. How sad to see the village, church and all, built up again brand-new, and whitewashed to the very steeple-top; - a new school at the town-end - a new crucifix by the wayside. How sad to see the old folk well clothed in the fabrics of England or Belgium, doing an easy trade in milk and fruit, because the land they till has become their own, and not the prince's; while their sons are thriving farmers on the prairies of the far West. Very unpicturesque, no doubt, is wealth and progress, peace and safety, cleanliness and comfort. But they possess advantages unknown to the Ancien Regime, which was, if nothing else, picturesque. Men could paint amusing and often pretty pictures of its people and its places.

Consider that word, "picturesque." It, and the notion of art which it expresses, are the children of the Ancien Regime - of the era of decay. The healthy, vigorous, earnest, progressive Middle Age never dreamed of admiring, much less of painting, for their own sake, rags and ruins; the fashion sprang up at the end of the seventeenth century; it lingered on during the first quarter of our century, kept alive by the reaction from 1815-25. It is all but dead now, before the return of vigorous and progressive thought. An admirer of the Middle Ages now does not build a sham ruin in his grounds; he restores a church, blazing with colour, like a medieval illumination. He has learnt to look on that which went by the name of picturesque in his great-grandfather's time, as an old Greek or a Middle Age monk would have done - as something squalid, ugly, a sign of neglect, disease, death; and therefore to be hated and abolished, if it cannot be restored. At Carcassone, now, M. Viollet-le-Duc, under the auspices of the Emperor of the French, is spending his vast learning, and much money, simply in abolishing the picturesque; in restoring stone for stone, each member of that wonderful museum of Middle Age architecture: Roman, Visigothic, Moslem, Romaine, Early English, later French, all is being reproduced exactly as it must have existed centuries since. No doubt that is not the highest function of art: but it is a preparation for the highest, a step toward some future creative school. As the early Italian artists, by careful imitation, absorbed into their minds the beauty and meaning of old Greek and Roman art; so must the artists of our days by the art of the Middle Age and the Renaissance. They must learn to copy, before they can learn to surpass; and, meanwhile, they must learn - indeed they have learnt - that decay is ugliness, and the imitation of decay, a making money out of the public shame.

The picturesque sprang up, as far as I can discover, suddenly, during the time of exhaustion and recklessness which followed the great struggles of the sixteenth century. Salvator Rosa and Callot, two of the earliest professors of picturesque art, have never been since surpassed. For indeed, they drew from life. The rags and the ruins, material, and alas! spiritual, were all around them; the lands and the creeds alike lay waste. There was ruffianism and misery among the masses of Europe; unbelief and artificiality among the upper classes; churches and monasteries defiled, cities sacked, farmsteads plundered and ruinate, and all the wretchedness which Callot has immortalised - for a warning to evil rulers - in his Miseres de la Guerre. The world was all gone wrong: but as for setting it right again - who could do that? And so men fell into a sentimental regret for the past, and its beauties, all exaggerated by the foreshortening of time; while they wanted strength or faith to reproduce it. At last they became so accustomed to the rags and ruins, that they looked on them as the normal condition of humanity, as the normal field for painters.

Only now and then, and especially toward the latter half of the eighteenth century, when thought began to revive, and men dreamed of putting the world to rights once more, there rose before them glimpses of an Arcadian ideal. Country life - the primaeval calling of men - how graceful and pure it might be! How graceful - if not pure - it once had been! The boors of Teniers and the beggars of Murillo might be true to present fact; but there was a fairer ideal, which once had been fact, in the Eclogues of Theocritus, and the Loves of Daphnis and Chloe. And so men took to dreaming of shepherds and shepherdesses, and painting them on canvas, and modelling them in china, according to their cockney notions of what they had been once, and always ought to be. We smile now at Sevres and Dresden shepherdesses; but the wise man will surely see in them a certain pathos. They indicated a craving after something better than boorishness; and the many men and women may have become the gentler and purer by looking even at them, and have said sadly to themselves: "Such might have been the peasantry of half Europe, had it not been for devastations of the Palatinate, wars of succession, and the wicked wills of emperors and kings."

LECTURE III - THE EXPLOSIVE FORCES

In a former lecture in this Institution, I said that the human race owed more to the eighteenth century than to any century since the Christian era. It may seem a bold assertion to those who value duly the century which followed the revival of Greek literature, and consider that the eighteenth century was but the child, or rather grandchild, thereof. But I must persist in my opinion, even though it seem to be inconsistent with my description of the very same era as one of decay and death. For side by side with the death, there was manifold fresh birth; side by side with the decay there was active growth; - side by side with them, fostered by them, though generally in strong opposition to them, whether conscious or unconscious. We must beware, however, of trying to find between that decay and that growth a bond of cause and effect where there is really none. The general decay may have determined the course of many men's thoughts; but it no more set them thinking than (as I have heard said) the decay of the Ancien Regime produced the new Regime - a loose metaphor, which, like all metaphors, will not hold water, and must not be taken for a philosophic truth. That would be to confess man - what I shall never confess him to be - the creature of circumstances; it would be to fall into the same fallacy of spontaneous generation as did the ancients, when they believed that bees were bred from the carcass of a dead ox. In the first place, the bees were no bees, but flies - unless when some true swarm of honey bees may have taken up their abode within the empty ribs, as Samson's bees did in that of the lion. But bees or flies, each sprang from an egg, independent of the carcass, having a vitality of its own: it was fostered by the carcass it fed on during development; but bred from it it was not, any more than Marat was bred from the decay of the Ancien Regime. There are flies which, by feeding on putridity, become poisonous themselves, as did Marat: but even they owe their vitality and organisation to something higher than that on which they feed; and each of them, however, defaced and debased, was at first a "thought of God." All true manhood consists in the defiance of circumstances; and if any man be the creature of circumstances, it is because he has become so, like the drunkard; because he has ceased to be a man, and sunk downward toward the brute.

Accordingly we shall find, throughout the 18th century, a stirring of thought, an originality, a resistance to circumstances, an indignant defiance of circumstances, which would have been impossible, had circumstances been the true lords and shapers of mankind. Had that latter been the case, the downward progress of the Ancien Regime would have been irremediable. Each generation, conformed more and more to the element in which it lived, would have sunk deeper in dull acquiescence to evil, in ignorance of all cravings save those of the senses; and if at any time intolerable wrong or want had driven it to revolt, it would have issued, not in the proclamation of new and vast ideas, but in an anarchic struggle for revenge and bread.

There are races, alas! which seem, for the present at

least, mastered by circumstances. Some, like the Chinese, have sunk back into that state; some, like the negro in Africa, seem not yet to have emerged from it; but in Europe, during the eighteenth century, were working not merely new forces and vitalities (abstractions which mislead rather than explain), but living persons in plenty, men and women, with independent and original hearts and brains, instinct, in spite of all circumstances, with power which we shall most wisely ascribe directly to Him who is the Lord and Giver of Life.

Such persons seemed - I only say seemed - most numerous in England and in Germany. But there were enough of them in France to change the destiny of that great nation for awhile - perhaps for ever.

M. de Tocqueville has a whole chapter, and a very remarkable one, which appears at first sight to militate against my belief - a chapter "showing that France was the country in which men had become most alike."

"The men," he says, "of that time, especially those belonging to the upper and middle ranks of society, who alone were at all conspicuous, were all exactly alike."

And it must be allowed, that if this were true of the upper and middle classes, it must have been still more true of the mass of the lowest population, who, being most animal, are always most moulded - or rather crushed - by their own circumstances, by public opinion, and by the wants of five senses, common to all alike.

But when M. de Tocqueville attributes this curious fact

to the circumstances of their political state - to that "government of one man which in the end has the inevitable effect of rendering all men alike, and all mutually indifferent to their common fate" - we must differ, even from him: for facts prove the impotence of that, or of any other circumstance, in altering the hearts and souls of men, in producing in them anything but a mere superficial and temporary resemblance.

For all the while there was, among these very French, here and there a variety of character and purpose, sufficient to burst through that very despotism, and to develop the nation into manifold, new, and quite original shapes. Thus it was proved that the uniformity had been only in their outside crust and shell. What tore the nation to pieces during the Reign of Terror, but the boundless variety and originality of the characters which found themselves suddenly in free rivalry? What else gave to the undisciplined levies, the bankrupt governments, the parvenu heroes of the Republic, a manifold force, a self-dependent audacity, which made them the conquerors, and the teachers (for good and evil) of the civilised world? If there was one doctrine which the French Revolution specially proclaimed - which it caricatured till it brought it into temporary disrepute - it was this: that no man is like another; that in each is a God-given "individuality," an independent soul, which no government or man has a right to crush, or can crush in the long run: but which ought to have, and must have, a "carriere ouverte aux talents," freely to do the best for itself in the battle of life. The French Revolution, more than any event since twelve poor men set forth to convert the world some eighteen hundred years ago, proves that man ought not to be, and need not be, the creature of circumstances, the puppet of institutions; but, if he will, their conqueror and their lord.

Of these original spirits who helped to bring life out of death, and the modern world out of the decay of the mediaeval world, the French PHILOSOPHES and encyclopaedists are, of course, the most notorious. They confessed, for the most part, that their original inspiration had come from England. They were, or considered themselves, the disciples of Locke; whose philosophy, it seems to me, their own acts disproved.

And first, a few words on these same philosophes. One may be thoroughly aware of their deficiencies, of their sins, moral as well as intellectual; and yet one may demand that everyone should judge them fairly - which can only be done by putting himself in their place; and any fair judgment of them will, I think, lead to the conclusion that they were not mere destroyers, inflamed with hate of everything which mankind had as yet held sacred. Whatever sacred things they despised, one sacred thing they reverenced, which men had forgotten more and more since the seventeenth century - common justice and common humanity. It was this, I believe, which gave them their moral force. It was this which drew towards them the hearts, not merely of educated bourgeois and nobles (on the menu peuple they had no influence, and did not care to have any), but of every continental sovereign who felt in himself higher aspirations than those of a mere selfish tyrant - Frederick the Great, Christina of Sweden, Joseph of Austria, and even that fallen Juno, Catharine of Russia, with all her sins. To take the most extreme instance - Voltaire. We may question his being a philosopher at all. We may deny that he had even a tincture of formal philosophy. We may doubt much whether he had any of that human and humorous common sense, which is often a good substitute for the philosophy of the schools. We may feel against him a just and honest indignation when we remember that he dared to travestie into a foul satire the tale of his country's purest and noblest heroine; but we must recollect, at the same time, that he did a public service to the morality of his own country, and of all Europe, by his indignation - quite as just and honest as any which we may feel - at the legal murder of Calas. We must recollect that, if he exposes baseness and foulness with too cynical a license of speech (in which, indeed, he sinned no more than had the average of French writers since the days of Montaigne), he at least never advocates them, as did Le Sage. We must recollect that, scattered throughout his writings, are words in favour of that which is just, merciful, magnanimous, and even, at times, in favour of that which is pure; which proves that in Voltaire, as in most men, there was a double self - the one sickened to cynicism by the iniquity and folly which he saw around him - the other, hungering after a nobler life, and possibly exciting that hunger in one and another, here and there, who admired him for other reasons than the educated mob, which cried after him "Vive la Pucelle."

Rousseau, too. Easy it is to feel disgust, contempt, for the "Confessions" and the "Nouvelle Heloise" - for much, too much, in the man's own life and character. One would think the worse of the young Englishman who did not so feel, and express his feelings roundly and roughly. But all young Englishmen should recollect, that to Rousseau's "Emile" they owe their deliverance from the useless pedantries, the degrading brutalities, of the medieval system of school education; that "Emile" awakened throughout civilised Europe a conception of education just, humane, rational, truly scientific, because founded upon facts; that if it had not been written by one writhing under the bitter consequences of mis-education, and feeling their sting and their brand day by day on his own spirit, Miss Edgeworth might never have reformed our nurseries, or Dr. Arnold our public schools.

And so with the rest of the philosophes. That there were charlatans among them, vain men, pretentious men, profligate men, selfish, self-seeking, and hypocritical men, who doubts? Among what class of men were there not such in those evil days? In what class of men are there not such now, in spite of all social and moral improvement? But nothing but the conviction, among the average, that they were in the right - that they were fighting a battle for which it was worth while to dare, and if need be to suffer, could have enabled them to defy what was then public opinion, backed by overwhelming physical force.

Their intellectual defects are patent. No one can deny that their inductions were hasty and partial: but then they were inductions as opposed to the dull pedantry of the schools, which rested on tradition only half believed, or pretended to be believed. No one can deny that their theories were too general and abstract; but then they were theories as opposed to the no-theory of the Ancien Regime, which was, "Let us eat and drink, for to-morrow we die."

Theories - principles - by them if men do not live, by them men are, at least, stirred into life, at the sight of something more noble than themselves. Only by great ideas, right or wrong, could such a world as that which Le Sage painted, be roused out of its slough of foul self-satisfaction, and equally foul self-discontent.

For mankind is ruled and guided, in the long run, not by practical considerations, not by self-interest, not by compromises; but by theories and principles, and those of the most abstruse, delicate, supernatural, and literally unspeakable kind; which, whether they be according to reason or not, are so little according to logic - that is, to speakable reason - that they cannot be put into speech. Men act, whether singly or in masses, by impulses and instincts for which they give reasons quite incompetent, often quite irrelevant; but which they have caught from each other, as they catch fever or small-pox; as unconsciously, and yet as practically and potently; just as the nineteenth century has caught from the philosophers of the eighteenth most practical rules of conduct, without even (in most cases) having read a word of their works.

And what has this century caught from these philosophers? One rule it has learnt, and that a most practical one - to appeal in all cases, as much as possible, to "Reason and the Laws of Nature." That, at least, the philosophers tried to do. Often they failed. Their conceptions of reason and of the laws of nature being often incorrect, they appealed to unreason and to laws which were not those of nature. "The fixed idea of them all was," says M. de Tocqueville, "to substitute simple and elementary rules, deduced from reason and natural law, for the complicated traditional customs which governed the society of their time." They were often rash, hasty, in the application of their method. They ignored whole classes of facts, which, though spiritual and not physical, are just as much facts, and facts for science, as those which concern a stone or a fungus. They mistook for merely complicated traditional customs, many most sacred institutions which were just as much founded on reason and natural law, as any theories of their own. But who shall say that their method was not correct? That it was not the only method? They appealed to reason. Would you have had them appeal to unreason? They appealed to natural law. Would you have had them appeal to unnatural law? - law according to which God did not make this world? Alas! that had been done too often already. Solomon saw it done in his time, and called it folly, to which he prophesied no good end. Rabelais saw it done in his time; and wrote his chapters on the "Children of Physis and the Children of Antiphysis." But, born in an evil generation, which was already, even in 1500, ripening for the revolution of 1789, he was sensual and, I fear, cowardly enough to hide his light, not under a bushel, but under a dunghill; till men took him for a jester of jests; and his great wisdom was lost to the worse and more foolish generations which followed him, and thought they understood him.

But as for appealing to natural law for that which is good for men, and to reason for the power of discerning that same good - if man cannot find truth by that method, by what method shall he find it?

And thus it happened that, though these philosophers and encyclopaedists were not men of science, they were at least the heralds and the coadjutors of science.

We may call them, and justly, dreamers, theorists, fanatics. But we must recollect that one thing they meant to do, and did. They recalled men to facts; they bid them ask of everything they saw - What are the facts of the case? Till we know the facts, argument is worse than useless.

Now the habit of asking for the facts of the case must

deliver men more or less from that evil spirit which the old Romans called "Fama;" from her whom Virgil described in the AEneid as the ugliest, the falsest, and the cruellest of monsters.

From "Fama;" from rumours, hearsays, exaggerations, scandals, superstitions, public opinions - whether from the ancient public opinion that the sun went round the earth, or the equally public opinion, that those who dared to differ from public opinion were hateful to the deity, and therefore worthy of death - from all these blasts of Fame's lying trumpet they helped to deliver men; and they therefore helped to insure something like peace and personal security for those quiet, modest, and generally virtuous men, who, as students of physical science, devoted their lives, during the eighteenth century, to asking of nature - What are the facts of the case?

It was no coincidence, but a connection of cause and effect, that during the century of philosopher sound physical science throve, as she had never thriven before; that in zoology and botany, chemistry and medicine, geology and astronomy, man after man, both of the middle and the noble classes, laid down on more and more sound, because more and more extended foundations, that physical science which will endure as an everlasting heritage to mankind; endure, even though a second Byzantine period should reduce it to a timid and traditional pedantry, or a second irruption of barbarians sweep it away for awhile, to revive again (as classic philosophy revived in the fifteenth century) among new and more energetic races; when the kingdom of God shall have been taken away from us, and given to a nation bringing forth the fruits thereof.

An eternal heritage, I say, for the human race; which once gained, can never be lost; which stands, and will stand; marches, and will march, proving its growth, its health, its progressive force, its certainty of final victory, by those very changes, disputes, mistakes, which the ignorant and the bigoted hold up to scorn, as proofs of its uncertainty and its rottenness; because they never have dared or cared to ask boldly - What are the facts of the case? - and have never discovered either the acuteness, the patience, the calm justice, necessary for ascertaining the facts, or their awful and divine certainty when once ascertained.

[But these philosophers (it will be said) hated all religion.

Before that question can be fairly discussed, it is surely right to consider what form of religion that was which they found working round them in France, and on the greater part of the Continent. The quality thereof may have surely had something to do (as they themselves asserted) with that "sort of rage" with which (to use M. de Tocqueville's words) "the Christian religion was attacked in France."

M. de Tocqueville is of opinion (and his opinion is likely to be just) that "the Church was not more open to attack in France than elsewhere; that the corruptions and abuses which had been allowed to creep into it were less, on the contrary, there than in most Catholic countries. The Church of France was infinitely more tolerant than it ever had been previously, and than it still was among other nations. Consequently, the peculiar causes of this phenomenon" (the hatred which it aroused) "must be looked for less in the condition of religion than in that of society."

"We no longer," he says, shortly after, "ask in what the Church of that day erred as a religious institution, but how far it stood opposed to the political revolution which was at hand." And he goes on to show how the principles of her ecclesiastical government, and her political position, were such that the philosophes must needs have been her enemies. But he mentions another fact which seems to me to belong neither to the category of religion nor to that of politics; a fact which, if he had done us the honour to enlarge upon it, might have led him and his readers to a more true understanding of the disrepute into which Christianity had fallen in France.

"The ecclesiastical authority had been specially employed in keeping watch over the progress of thought; and the censorship of books was a daily annoyance to the philosophes. By defending the common liberties of the human mind against the Church, they were combating in their own cause: and they began by breaking the shackles which pressed most closely on themselves."

Just so. And they are not to be blamed if they pressed first and most earnestly reforms which they knew by painful experience to be necessary. All reformers are wont thus to begin at home. It is to their honour if, not content with shaking off their own fetters, they begin to see that others are fettered likewise; and, reasoning from the particular to the universal, to learn that their own cause is the cause of mankind.

There is, therefore, no reason to doubt that these men were honest, when they said that they were combating, not in their own cause merely, but in that of humanity; and that the Church was combating in her own cause, and that of her power and privilege. The Church replied that she, too, was combating for humanity; for its moral and eternal well-being. But that is just what the philosophes denied. They said (and it is but fair to take a statement which appears on the face of all their writings; which is the one key-note on which they ring perpetual changes), that the cause of the Church in France was not that of humanity, but of inhumanity; not that of nature, but of unnature; not even that of grace, but of disgrace. Truely or falsely, they complained that the French clergy had not only identified themselves with the repression of free thought, and of physical science, especially that of the Newtonian astronomy, but that they had proved themselves utterly unfit, for centuries past, to exercise any censorship whatsoever over the thoughts of men: that they had identified themselves with the cause of darkness, not of light; with persecution and torture, with the dragonnades of Louis XIV., with the murder of Calas and of Urban Grandier; with celibacy, hysteria, demonology, witchcraft, and the shameful public scandals, like those of Gauffredi, Grandier, and Pere Giraud, which had arisen out of mental disease; with forms of worship which seemed to them (rightly or wrongly) idolatry, and miracles which seemed to them (rightly or wrongly) impostures; that the clergy interfered perpetually with the sanctity of family life, as well as with the welfare of the state; that their evil counsels, and specially those of the Jesuits, had been patent and potent causes of much of the misrule and misery of Louis XIV.'s and XV.'s reigns; and that with all these heavy counts against them, their morality was not such as to make other men more moral; and was not - at least among the hierarchy - improving, or likely to improve. To a Mazarin, a De Retz, a Richelieu (questionable men enough) had succeeded a

Dubois, a Rohan, a Lomenie de Brienne, a Maury, a Talleyrand; and at the revolution of 1789 thoughtful Frenchmen asked, once and for all, what was to be done with a Church of which these were the hierophants?

Whether these complaints affected the French Church as a "religious" institution, must depend entirely on the meaning which is attached to the word "religion": that they affected her on scientific, rational, and moral grounds, independent of any merely political one, is as patent as that the attack based on them was one-sided, virulent, and often somewhat hypocritical, considering the private morals of many of the assailants. We know - or ought to know - that within that religion which seemed to the philosophes (so distorted and defaced had it become) a nightmare dream, crushing the life out of mankind, there lie elements divine, eternal; necessary for man in this life and the life to come. But we are bound to ask - Had they a fair chance of knowing what we know? Have we proof that their hatred was against all religion, or only against that which they saw around them? Have we proof that they would have equally hated, had they been in permanent contact with them, creeds more free from certain faults which seemed to them, in the case of the French Church, ineradicable and inexpiable? Till then we must have charity - which is justice - even for the philosophes of the eighteenth century.

This view of the case had been surely overlooked by M. de Tocqueville, when he tried to explain by the fear of revolutions, the fact that both in America and in England, "while the boldest political doctrines of the eighteenth-century philosophers have been adopted, their anti-religious doctrines have made no way."

He confesses that, "Among the English, French irreligious philosophy had been preached, even before the greater part of the French philosophers were born. It was Bolingbroke who set up Voltaire. Throughout the eighteenth century infidelity had celebrated champions in England. Able writers and profound thinkers espoused that cause, but they were never able to render it triumphant as in France." Of these facts there can be no doubt: but the cause which he gives for the failure of infidelity will surely sound new and strange to those who know the English literature and history of that century. It was, he says, "inasmuch as all those who had anything to fear from revolutions, eagerly came to the rescue of the established faith." Surely there was no talk of revolutions; no wish, expressed or concealed, to overthrow either government or society, in the aristocratic clique to whom English infidelity was confined. Such was, at least, the opinion of Voltaire, who boasted that "All the works of the modern philosophers together would never make as much noise in the world as was made in former days by the disputes of the Cordeliers about the shape of their sleeves and hoods." If (as M. de Tocqueville says) Bolingbroke set up Voltaire, neither master nor pupil had any more leaning than Hobbes had toward a democracy which was not dreaded in those days because it had never been heard of. And if (as M. de Tocqueville heartily allows) the English apologists of Christianity triumphed, at least for the time being, the cause of their triumph must be sought in the plain fact that such men as Berkeley, Butler, and Paley, each according to his light, fought the battle fairly, on the common ground of reason and philosophy, instead of on that of tradition and authority; and that the forms of Christianity current in England - whether Quaker, Puritan, or Anglican - offended, less than that current in France, the common-sense and the human instincts of the many, or of the sceptics themselves.]

But the eighteenth century saw another movement, all the more powerful, perhaps, because it was continually changing its shape, even its purpose; and gaining fresh life and fresh adherents with every change. Propagated at first by men of the school of Locke, it became at last a protest against the materialism of that school, on behalf of all that is, or calls itself, supernatural and mysterious. Abjuring, and honestly, all politics, it found itself sucked into the political whirlpool in spite of itself, as all human interests which have any life in them must be at last. It became an active promoter of the Revolution; then it helped to destroy the Revolution, when that had, under Napoleon, become a levelling despotism; then it helped, as actively, to keep revolutionary principles alive, after the reaction of 1815: - a Protean institution, whose power we in England are as apt to undervalue as the governments of the Continent were apt, during the eighteenth century, to exaggerate it. I mean, of course, Freemasonry, and the secret societies which, honestly and honourably disowned by Freemasonry, yet have either copied it, or actually sprung out of it. In England, Freemasonry never was, it seems, more than a liberal and respectable benefit-club; for secret societies are needless for any further purposes, amid free institutions and a free press. But on the Continent during the eighteenth century, Freemasonry excited profound suspicion and fear on the part of statesmen who knew perfectly well their friends from their foes; and whose precautions were, from their point of view, justified by the results.

I shall not enter into the deep question of the origin of

Freemasonry. One uninitiate, as I am, has no right to give an opinion on the great questions of the mediaeval lodge of Kilwinning and its Scotch degrees; on the seven Templars, who, after poor Jacques Molay was burnt at Paris, took refuge on the Isle of Mull, in Scotland, found there another Templar and brother Mason, ominously named Harris; took to the trowel in earnest, and revived the Order; - on the Masons who built Magdeburg Cathedral in 876; on the English Masons assembled in Pagan times by "St. Albone, that worthy knight;" on the revival of English Masonry by Edwin, son of Athelstan; on Magnus Grecus, who had been at the building of Solomon's Temple, and taught Masonry to Charles Martel; on the pillars Jachin and Boaz; on the masonry of Hiram of Tyre, and indeed of Adam himself, of whose first fig-leaf the masonic apron may be a type - on all these matters I dare no more decide than on the making of the Trojan Horse, the birth of Romulus and Remus, or the incarnation of Vishnoo.

All I dare say is, that Freemasonry emerges in its present form into history and fact, seemingly about the beginning of George I.'s reign, among Englishmen and noblemen, notably in four lodges in the city of London: (1) at The Goose and Gridiron alehouse in St. Paul's Churchyard; (2) at The Crown alehouse near Drury Lane; (3) at The Apple Tree tavern near Covent Garden; (4) at The Rummer and Grapes tavern, in Charnel Row, Westminster. That its principles were brotherly love and good fellowship, which included in those days port, sherry, claret, and punch; that it was founded on the ground of mere humanity, in every sense of the word; being (as was to be expected from the temper of the times) both aristocratic and liberal, admitting to its ranks virtuous gentlemen "obliged,"

Charles Kingsley

says an old charge, "only to that religion wherein all men agree, leaving their particular opinions to themselves: that is, to be good men and true, or men of honour and honesty, by whatever denominations or persuasions they may be distinguished; whereby Masonry becomes the centre of union and means of conciliating true friendship among persons that otherwise must have remained at a distance."

Little did the honest gentlemen who established or re-established their society on these grounds, and fenced it with quaint ceremonies, old or new, conceive the importance of their own act; we, looking at it from a distance, may see all that such a society involved, which was quite new to the world just then; and see, that it was the very child of the Ancien Regime - of a time when men were growing weary of the violent factions, political and spiritual, which had torn Europe in pieces for more than a century, and longed to say: "After all, we are all alike in one thing - for we are at least men."

Its spread through England and Scotland, and the seceding bodies which arose from it, as well as the supposed Jacobite tendency of certain Scotch lodges, do not concern us here. The point interesting to us just now is, that Freemasonry was imported to the Continent exclusively by English and Scotch gentlemen and noblemen. Lord Derwentwater is said by some to have founded the "Loge Anglaise" in Paris in 1725; the Duke of Richmond one in his own castle of Aubigny shortly after. It was through Hanoverian influence that the movement seems to have spread into Germany. In 1733, for instance, the English Grand Master, Lord Strathmore, permitted eleven German gentlemen and good brethren to form a lodge in

Hamburg. Into this English Society was Frederick the Great, when Crown Prince, initiated, in spite of strict old Frederick William's objections, who had heard of it as an English invention of irreligious tendency. Francis I. of Austria was made a Freemason at the Hague, Lord Chesterfield being in the chair, and then became a Master in London under the name of "Brother Lothringen," to the discontent of Maria Theresa, whose woman's wit saw farther than her husband. Englishmen and Scotchmen introduced the new society into Russia and into Geneva. Sweden and Poland seem to have received it from France; while, in the South, it seems to have been exclusively an English plant. Sackville, Duke of Middlesex, is said to have founded the first lodge at Florence in 1733, Lord Coleraine at Gibraltar and Madrid, one Gordon in Portugal; and everywhere, at the commencement of the movement, we find either London or Scotland the mother-lodges, introducing on the Continent those liberal and humane ideas of which England was then considered, to her glory, as the only home left on earth.

But, alas! the seed sown grew up into strange shapes, according to the soil in which it rooted. False doctrine, heresy, and schism, according to Herr Findel, the learned and rational historian whom I have chiefly followed, defiled the new Church from its infancy. "In France," so he bemoans himself, "first of all there shot up that baneful seed of lies and frauds, of vanity and presumption, of hatred and discord, the mischievous high degrees; the misstatement that our order was allied to the Templars, and existed at the time of the Crusades; the removal of old charges, the bringing in surreptitiously of a multitude of symbols and forms which awoke the love of secrecy; knighthood; and, in fact, all which tended to poison Freemasonry." Herr

Findel seems to attribute these evils principally to the "high degrees." It would have been more simple to have attributed them to the morals of the French noblesse in the days of Louis Quinze. What could a corrupt tree bring forth, but corrupt fruit? If some of the early lodges, like those of "La Felicite" and "L'Ancre," to which women were admitted, resembled not a little the Bacchic mysteries of old Rome, and like them called for the interference of the police, still no great reform was to be expected, when those Sovereign Masonic Princes, the "Emperors of the East and West," quarrelled - knights of the East against knights of the West - till they were absorbed or crushed by the Lodge "Grand Orient," with Philippe Egalite, Duc de Chartres, as their grand master, and as his representative, the hero of the diamond necklace, and disciple of Count Cagliostro - Louis, Prince de Rohan.

But if Freemasonry, among the frivolous and sensual French noblesse, became utterly frivolous and sensual itself, it took a deeper, though a questionably fantastic form, among the more serious and earnest German nobility. Forgetful as they too often were of their duty to their peoples - tyrannical, extravagant, debauched by French opinions, French fashions, French luxuries, till they had begun to despise their native speech, their native literature, almost their native land, and to hide their native homeliness under a clumsy varnish of French outside civilisation, which the years 1807-13 rubbed off them again with a brush of iron - they were yet Germans at heart; and that German instinct for the unseen - call it enthusiasm, mysticism, what you will, you cannot make it anything but a human fact, and a most powerful, and (as I hold) most blessed fact - that instinct for the unseen, I say, which gives peculiar value to German philosophy, poetry, art, religion, and above all to German family life, and which is just the complement needed to prevent our English common-sense, matter-of-fact Lockism from degenerating into materialism - that was only lying hidden, but not dead, in the German spirit.

With the Germans, therefore, Freemasonry assumed a nobler and more earnest shape. Dropping, very soon, that Lockite and Philosophe tone which had perhaps recommended it to Frederick the Great in his youth, it became mediaevalist and mystic. It craved after a resuscitation of old chivalrous spirit, and the virtues of the knightly ideal, and the old German biederkeit und tapferkeit, which were all defiled and overlaid by French fopperies. And not in vain; as no struggle after a noble aim, however confused or fantastic, is ever in vain. Freemasonry was the direct parent of the Tugenbund, and of those secret societies which freed Germany from Napoleon. Whatever follies young members of them may have committed; whatever Jahn and his Turnerei; whatever the iron youths, with their iron decorations and iron boot-heels; whatever, in a word, may have been said or done amiss, in that childishness which (as their own wisest writers often lament) so often defaces the noble childlikeness of the German spirit, let it be always remembered that under the impulse first given by Freemasonry, as much as that given by such heroes as Stein and Scharnhorst, Germany shook off the chains which had fallen on her in her sleep; and stood once more at Leipsic, were it but for a moment, a free people alike in body and in soul.

Remembering this, and the solid benefits which Germany owed to Masonic influences, one shrinks from saying much of the extravagances in which its

Masonry indulged before the French Revolution. Yet they are so characteristic of the age, so significant to the student of human nature, that they must be hinted at, though not detailed.

It is clear that Masonry was at first a movement confined to the aristocracy, or at least to the most educated classes; and clear, too, that it fell in with a temper of mind unsatisfied with the dry dogmatism into which the popular creeds had then been frozen - unsatisfied with their own Frenchified foppery and pseudo-philosophy - unsatisfied with want of all duty, purpose, noble thought, or noble work. With such a temper of mind it fell in: but that very temper was open (as it always is) to those dreams of a royal road to wisdom and to virtue, which have haunted, in all ages, the luxurious and the idle.

Those who will, may read enough, and too much, of the wonderful secrets in nature and science and theosophy, which men expected to find and did not find in the higher degrees of Masonry, till old Voss - the translator of Homer - had to confess, that after "trying for eleven years to attain a perfect knowledge of the inmost penetralia, where the secret is said to be, and of its invisible guardians," all he knew was that "the documents which he had to make known to the initiated were nothing more than a well got-up farce."

But the mania was general. The high-born and the virtuous expected to discover some panacea for their own consciences in what Voss calls, "A multitude of symbols, which are ever increasing the farther you penetrate, and are made to have a moral application through some arbitrary twisting of their meaning, as if I were to attempt expounding the chaos on my writing-desk."

A rich harvest-field was an aristocracy in such a humour, for quacks of every kind; richer even than that of France, in that the Germans were at once more honest and more earnest, and therefore to be robbed more easily. The carcass was there: and the birds of prey were gathered together.

Of Rosa, with his lodge of the Three Hammers, and his Potsdam gold-making; - of Johnson, alias Leuchte, who passed himself off as a Grand Prior sent from Scotland to resuscitate the order of Knights Templars; who informed his disciples that the Grand Master Von Hund commanded 26,000 men; that round the convent (what convent, does not appear) a high wall was erected, which was guarded day and night; that the English navy was in the hands of the Order; that they had MSS. written by Hugo de Paganis (a mythic hero who often figures in these fables); that their treasure was in only three places in the world, in Ballenstadt, in the icy mountains of Savoy, and in China; that whosoever drew on himself the displeasure of the Order, perished both body and soul; who degraded his rival Rosa to the sound of military music, and after having had, like every dog, his day, died in prison in the Wartburg; - of the Rosicrucians, who were accused of wanting to support and advance the Catholic religion - one would think the accusation was very unnecessary, seeing that their actual dealings were with the philosopher's stone, and the exorcism of spirits: and that the first apostle of the new golden Rosicrucian order, one Schropfer, getting into debt, and fearing exposure, finished his life in an altogether un-catholic manner at Leipsic in 1774, by shooting himself; - of Keller and his Urim and Thummim; - of

Wollner (who caught the Crown Prince Frederick William) with his three names of Chrysophiron, Heliconus, and Ophiron, and his fourth name of Ormesus Magnus, under which all the brethren were to offer up for him solemn prayers and intercessions; - of Baron Heinrich von Ekker and Eckenhofen, gentleman of the bed-chamber and counsellor of the Duke of Coburg Saalfeld, and his Jewish colleague Hirschmann, with their Asiatic brethren and order named Ben Bicca, Cabalistic and Talmudic; of the Illuminati, and poor Adam Weisshaupt, Professor of Canon and National Law at Ingoldstadt in Bavaria, who set up what he considered an Anti-Jesuitical order on a Jesuit model, with some vague hope, according to his own showing, of "perfecting the reasoning powers interesting to mankind, spreading the knowledge of sentiments both humane and social, checking wicked inclinations, standing up for oppressed and suffering virtue against all wrong, promoting the advancement of men of merit, and in every way facilitating the acquirement of knowledge and science;" - of this honest silly man, and his attempts to carry out all his fine projects by calling himself Spartacus, Bavaria Achaia, Austria Egypt, Vienna Rome, and so forth; - of Knigge, who picked his honest brains, quarrelled with him, and then made money and fame out of his plans, for as long as they lasted; - of Bode, the knight of the lilies of the valley, who, having caught Duke Ernest of Saxe Gotha, was himself caught by Knigge, and his eight, nine, or more ascending orders of unwisdom; - and finally of the Jesuits who, really with considerable excuses for their severity, fell upon these poor foolish Illuminati in 1784 throughout Bavaria, and had them exiled or imprisoned; - of all this you may read in the pages of Dr. Findel, and in many another book. For, forgotten as they are now, they made noise enough in their time.

And so it befell, that this eighteenth century, which is usually held to be the most "materialistic" of epochs, was, in fact, a most "spiritualistic" one; in which ghosts, demons, quacks, philosophers' stones, enchanters' wands, mysteries and mummeries, were as fashionable - as they will probably be again some day.

You have all heard of Cagliostro - "pupil of the sage Althotas, foster-child of the Scheriff of Mecca, probable son of the last king of Trebizond; named also Acharat, and 'Unfortunate child of Nature;' by profession healer of diseases, abolisher of wrinkles, friend of the poor and impotent; grand-master of the Egyptian Mason-lodge of High Science, spirit-summoner, gold-cook, Grand-Cophta, prophet, priest, Thaumaturgic moralist, and swindler" - born Giuseppe Balsamo of Palermo; - of him, and of his lovely Countess Seraphina - nee Lorenza Feliciani? You have read what Goethe - and still more important, what Mr. Carlyle has written on him, as on one of the most significant personages of the age? Remember, then, that Cagliostro was no isolated phenomenon; that his success - nay, his having even conceived the possibility of success in the brain that lay within that "brass-faced, bull-necked, thick-lipped" head - was made possible by public opinion. Had Cagliostro lived in our time, public opinion would have pointed out to him other roads to honour - on which he would doubtless have fared as well. For when the silly dace try to be caught and hope to be caught, he is a foolish pike who cannot gorge them. But the method most easy for a pike-nature like Cagliostro's, was in the eighteenth century, as it may be in the latter half of the nineteenth, to trade, in a materialist age, on the unsatisfied spiritual cravings of mankind. For what do all these phantasms betoken, but a generation ashamed of its own materialism, sensuality, insincerity, ignorance, and striving to escape therefrom by any and every mad superstition which seemed likely to give an answer to the awful questions - What are we, and where? and to lay to rest those instincts of the unseen and infinite around it, which tormented it like ghosts by day and night: a sight ludicrous or pathetic, according as it is looked on by a cynical or a human spirit.

It is easy to call such a phenomenon absurd, improbable. It is rather rational, probable, say certain to happen. Rational, I say; for the reason of man tells him, and has always told him, that he is a supernatural being, if by nature is meant that which is cognisable by his five senses: that his coming into this world, his relation to it, his exit from it - which are the three most important facts about him - are supernatural, not to be explained by any deductions from the impressions of his senses. And I make bold to say, that the recent discoveries of physical science - notably those of embryology - go only to justify that old and general belief of man. If man be told that the microscope and scalpel show no difference, in the first stage of visible existence, between him and the lower mammals, then he has a right to answer - as he will answer - So much the worse for the microscope and scalpel: so much the better for my old belief, that there is beneath my birth, life, death, a substratum of supernatural causes, imponderable, invisible, unknowable by any physical science whatsoever. If you cannot render me a reason how I came hither, and what I am, I must go to those who will render me one. And if that craving be not satisfied by a rational theory of life, it will demand satisfaction from some magical theory; as did the mind of the eighteenth century when, revolting from materialism, it fled to magic, to explain the ever-astounding miracle of life.

The old Regime. Will our age, in its turn, ever be spoken of as an old Regime? Will it ever be spoken of as a Regime at all; as an organised, orderly system of society and polity; and not merely as a chaos, an anarchy, a transitory struggle, of which the money-lender has been the real guide and lord?

But at least it will be spoken of as an age of progress, of rapid developments, of astonishing discoveries.

Are you so sure of that? There was an age of progress once. But what is our age - what is all which has befallen since 1815 - save after-swells of that great storm, which are weakening and lulling into heavy calm? Are we on the eve of stagnation? Of a long check to the human intellect? Of a new Byzantine era, in which little men will discuss, and ape, the deeds which great men did in their forefathers' days?

What progress - it is a question which some will receive with almost angry surprise - what progress has the human mind made since 1815?

If the thought be startling, do me the great honour of taking it home, and verifying for yourselves its truth or its falsehood. I do not say that it is altogether true. No proposition concerning human things, stated so broadly, can be. But see for yourselves, whether it is not at least more true than false; whether the ideas, the discoveries, of which we boast most in the nineteenth century, are not really due to the end of the eighteenth.

Whether other men did not labour, and we have only entered into their labours. Whether our positivist spirit, our content with the collecting of facts, our dread of vast theories, is not a symptom - wholesome, prudent, modest, but still a symptom - of our consciousness that we are not as our grandfathers were; that we can no longer conceive great ideas, which illumine, for good or evil, the whole mind and heart of man, and drive him on to dare and suffer desperately.

Railroads? Electric telegraphs? All honour to them in their place: but they are not progress; they are only the fruits of past progress. No outward and material thing is progress; no machinery causes progress; it merely spreads and makes popular the results of progress. Progress is inward, of the soul. And, therefore, improved constitutions, and improved book instruction - now miscalled education - are not progress: they are at best only fruits and signs thereof. For they are outward, material; and progress, I say, is inward. The self-help and self-determination of the independent soul - that is the root of progress; and the more human beings who have that, the more progress there is in the world. Give me a man who, though he can neither read nor write, yet dares think for himself, and do the thing he believes: that man will help forward the human race more than any thousand men who have read, or written either, a thousand books apiece, but have not dared to think for themselves. And better for his race, and better, I believe, in the sight of God, the confusions and mistakes of that one sincere brave man, than the second-hand and cowardly correctness of all the thousand.

As for the "triumphs of science," let us honour, with astonishment and awe, the genius of those who invented them; but let us remember that the things themselves are as a gun or a sword, with which we can kill our enemy, but with which also our enemy can kill us. Like all outward and material things, they are equally fit for good and for evil. In England here - they have been as yet, as far as I can see, nothing but blessings: but I have my very serious doubts whether they are likely to be blessings to the whole human race, for many an age to come. I can conceive them - may God avert the omen! - the instruments of a more crushing executive centralisation, of a more utter oppression of the bodies and souls of men, than the world has yet seen. I can conceive - may God avert the omen! - centuries hence, some future world-ruler sitting at the junction of all railroads, at the centre of all telegraph-wires - a world-spider in the omphalos of his world-wide web; and smiting from thence everything that dared to lift its head, or utter a cry of pain, with a swiftness and surety to which the craft of a Justinian or a Philip II. were but clumsy and impotent.

All, all outward things, be sure of it, are good or evil, exactly as far as they are in the hands of good men or of bad.

Moreover, paradoxical as it may seem, railroads and telegraphs, instead of inaugurating an era of progress, may possibly only retard it. "Rester sur un grand succes," which was Rossini's advice to a young singer who had achieved a triumph, is a maxim which the world often follows, not only from prudence, but from necessity. They have done so much that it seems neither prudent nor possible to do more. They will rest and be thankful.

Thus, gunpowder and printing made rapid changes

enough; but those changes had no farther development. The new art of war, the new art of literature, remained stationary, or rather receded and degenerated, till the end of the eighteenth century.

And so it may be with our means of locomotion and intercommunion, and what depends on them. The vast and unprecedented amount of capital, of social interest, of actual human intellect invested - I may say locked up - in these railroads, and telegraphs, and other triumphs of industry and science, will not enter into competition against themselves. They will not set themselves free to seek new discoveries in directions which are often actually opposed to their own, always foreign to it. If the money of thousands are locked up in these great works, the brains of hundreds of thousands, and of the very shrewdest too, are equally locked up therein likewise; and are to be subtracted from the gross material of social development, and added (without personal fault of their owners, who may be very good men) to the dead weight of vested selfishness, ignorance, and dislike of change.

Yes. A Byzantine and stationary age is possible yet. Perhaps we are now entering upon it; an age in which mankind shall be satisfied with the "triumphs of science," and shall look merely to the greatest comfort (call it not happiness) of the greatest number; and like the debased Jews of old, "having found the life of their hand, be therewith content," no matter in what mud-hole of slavery and superstition.

But one hope there is, and more than a hope - one certainty, that however satisfied enlightened public opinion may become with the results of science, and the progress of the human race, there will be always a more enlightened private opinion or opinions, which will not be satisfied therewith at all; a few men of genius, a few children of light, it may be a few persecuted, and a few martyrs for new truths, who will wish the world not to rest and be thankful, but to be discontented with itself, ashamed of itself, striving and toiling upward, without present hope of gain, till it has reached that unknown goal which Bacon saw afar off, and like all other heroes, died in faith, not having received the promises, but seeking still a polity which has foundations, whose builder and maker is God.

These will be the men of science, whether physical or spiritual. Not merely the men who utilise and apply that which is known (useful as they plainly are), but the men who themselves discover that which was unknown, and are generally deemed useless, if not hurtful, to their race. They will keep the sacred lamp burning unobserved in quiet studies, while all the world is gazing only at the gaslights flaring in the street. They will pass that lamp on from hand to hand, modestly, almost stealthily, till the day comes round again, when the obscure student shall be discovered once more to be, as he has always been, the strongest man on earth. For they follow a mistress whose footsteps may often slip, yet never fall; for she walks forward on the eternal facts of Nature, which are the acted will of God. A giantess she is; young indeed, but humble as yet: cautious and modest beyond her years. She is accused of trying to scale Olympus, by some who fancy that they have already scaled it themselves, and will, of course, brook no rival in their fancied monopoly of wisdom.

The accusation, I believe, is unjust. And yet science may scale Olympus after all. Without intending it, almost without knowing it, she may find herself hereafter upon a summit of which she never dreamed; surveying the universe of God in the light of Him who made it and her, and remakes them both for ever and ever. On that summit she may stand hereafter, if only she goes on, as she goes now, in humility and in patience; doing the duty which lies nearest her; lured along the upward road, not by ambition, vanity, or greed, but by reverent curiosity for every new pebble, and flower, and child, and savage, around her feet.

FOOTNOTES

{1} Mr. H. Reeve's translation of De Tocqueville's "France before the Revolution of 1789." p. 280.